CATS
OF THE WORLD
IN CROSS STITCH

CATS
OF THE WORLD
IN CROSS STITCH

Jayne Netley Mayhew and Nicki Wheeler

David & Charles

DEDICATION

To Ian, for every stitch that you felt
To Tim, for every word that you heard
Thanks for all your love and support

(Photograph on page 2)
All set for a delightful breakfast with a tea-cosy (see page 47),
cafétière cover (see page 44), egg cosies (see page 40), teaspoon (see
page 23) and jam pot cover (see page 25)

(Photograph on page 6)
The stunning leopard and tiger portraits (see page 60 and 66
respectively)

A DAVID & CHARLES BOOK

Text, designs and illustrations Copyright © Jayne Netley Mayhew 2000
Text Copyright © Jayne Netley Mayhew and Nicki Wheeler 2000
Photography and layout Copyright © David & Charles 2000

Jayne Netley Mayhew and Nicki Wheeler have asserted their right to be identified
as authors of this work in accordance with the Copyright, Designs and Patents
Act, 1988.

A catalogue record for this book is available from the British Library.

ISBN 0 7153 0941 2

Photography by Di Lewis
Book design by Glynis Edwards
Typeset by Glynis Edwards
and printed in Hong Kong by Di Nippon
for David & Charles
Brunel House   Newton Abbot   Devon

CONTENTS

INTRODUCTION

Large wild cats and smaller domestic cats are found all over the world, from parts of tropical Africa and Asia to snow-covered Greenland and Alaska. Domestic cats are the only members of the cat family to have adapted to living alongside humans. The domestic cats that we know and love today have all evolved from their larger wild relations and although they may vary in size, wild and domestic cats look alike and have similar characteristics.

Cats of the World in Cross Stitch, our fourth book, includes designs of wild and domestic cats from all areas of the world. The collection portrays the different personalities of cats — from the home-loving marmalade tom curled up on his favourite armchair to a regal lion surveying his territory. Many breeds and varieties are featured, from the common moggie to beautiful pedigree breeds and more exotic big cats. The designs are mixed throughout the book to show the variety of breeds and the similarities between the domestic and wild cats.

Each project is illustrated with beautiful colour photography, clear, full-colour charts and full stepped instructions for stitching and making up the items shown. A mixture of stranded cotton (floss) and tapestry wool (yarn) are used to work the projects using a variety of stitches including cross stitch, three-quarter cross stitch, half cross stitch, French knots and backstitch.

We have taken care to include a wide choice of designs suitable for stitchers of all abilities. For the beginner there is a selection of small designs including a Siamese kitten, butterflies, mice, goldfish and wandering paw prints. For the more experienced stitcher, a selection of large projects such as Lion Territory and Sitting Pretty would prove to be an enjoyable challenge, whilst the beautiful set of pictures representing the four seasons, showing a different cat and flower for each time of the year, would be enjoyable for stitchers of any level.

Some of the larger designs are flexible in that they can be stitched in either stranded cotton (floss) or tapestry wool (yarn) as they are worked in whole cross stitch and half cross stitch. These designs include the stunning tiger and leopard portraits which are shown worked in stranded cotton (floss) but with the colours for tapestry wool (yarn) also listed on the keys so that you can stitch them up in wool if you wish.

We hope that stitchers of all levels and abilities will enjoy stitching the many cats from this book as much as we enjoyed working on it. Some of the designs included are available as kit packs by Janlynn and can be obtained by mail order. Further details can be found in Stockists on page 127.

Happy Stitching

Jayne Netley Mayhew and Nicki Wheeler

Getting Started

Cross stitch is one of the most loved crafts around today and is still growing in popularity. One of the reasons for this, apart from it being so easy to work, is that the designs are simple to adapt. Merely by changing the type of thread, using a different fabric or background colour, a design can be transformed, and examples of this are given throughout the book. This section is a useful guide to the simple materials and equipment needed and to the basic techniques and stitches required.

MATERIALS

FABRICS

Most designs in this book have been worked on Aida fabric with 14 blocks or threads to one inch (2.5cm), often called 14-count. Some designs use a larger or smaller count Aida or an evenweave fabric such as linen. The same design stitched on fabrics of different counts will work up into different sizes. The larger the count (e.g. 18-count), the more threads per inch therefore the smaller the design. The smaller the count (e.g. 6-count), the fewer threads per inch therefore the larger the design. The finished size of each design is given but you can experiment by using different fabric counts to achieve surprising effects. Before starting a piece of work, always check the thread and stitch count to ensure that the design will fit the intended frame. Design size is easily calculated by dividing the stitch count by the fabric count.

Some of the designs are worked on very fine fabrics, such as the butterfly teaspoon on page 23. These can be very hard work on the eyes, so you could work the design using half cross stitch or use a slightly larger count Aida or evenweave fabric, which would make the design larger. Each project lists the type of fabric used, giving the thread count and fabric name, which should be quoted when purchasing goods. All DMC threads and fabrics can be obtained from good needlework shops or by mail order from the DMC catalogue and details of this can be found in Stockists on page 127.

THREADS

If you want your design to look exactly the same as those shown in the photographs, use the colours and threads listed for each project. The threads used in this book are DMC stranded cotton (floss) and tapestry wool (yarn).

Stranded cotton (floss) This is the most widely used embroidery thread and is available in hundreds of colour shades, including silver and gold metallic. It is a lustrous, mercerised thread which has a smooth finish and a slight sheen. It is made from six strands twisted together to form a thick thread which can be used whole or split into thinner strands. The type of fabric used will determine how many strands of thread you will need to use; most of the designs in this book use two strands of thread for cross stitch and one strand for backstitch.

Tapestry wool (yarn) DMC tapestry wool is a matt, hairy yarn made from 100% wool. It is made from short fibres twisted together to make a thick single thread which cannot be split. Designs are usually worked on canvas using one or two strands. A wide selection of colours is available and shades tend to be slightly duller than for stranded cotton (floss).

Thread Management Always keep threads tidy and manageable. Thread organisers and project cards are ideal for this purpose. Cut the threads into equal lengths and loop them into project cards with the thread shade code and colour key symbol written at the side. This will prevent threads from becoming tangled and the shade codes being lost.

EQUIPMENT

The equipment needed for successful cross stitching is minimal – another reason why the craft is so popular.

NEEDLES

Stitch your design using a tapestry needle which has a large eye and blunt end to prevent damage to the fabric. Choose a size of needle that will slide easily through the holes of the fabric without distorting or enlarging them. You will also need a sharp pair of embroidery scissors and will probably find sewing easier if you use a thimble, especially for projects stitched on canvas.

SCISSORS

You will need a sharp pair of embroidery scissors for cutting threads and a pair of dressmaking scissors for cutting fabric.

EMBROIDERY FRAMES

Your work will be easier to handle and stitches will be kept flat and smooth if you mount your fabric in an embroidery hoop or frame which will accommodate the whole design. There are various types available. If you use an embroidery hoop, bind the outer ring of the hoop with white bias tape to prevent it from marking the fabric. This will also keep the fabric taut and prevent it from slipping whilst working.

TECHNIQUES

Each project in this book includes a colour photograph of the worked design, a colour chart and key, instructions for making up the designs as gifts and accessories, and occasionally graphs and other diagrams. The following techniques and tips will help you achieve a professional finish by showing you how to prepare for work and care for your finished embroidery.

MEASUREMENTS

Each project gives the finished design size when worked on the recommended fabric, together with the amount of fabric needed. The fabric size stated is at least 8–10cm (3–4in) larger than the finished size of the design to allow for turnings or seam allowances when mounting the work or making it up into gifts. Measurements are given in metric with the imperial equivalent in brackets. Always use *either* metric or imperial – do not try to mix the two.

CENTRE POINT

To ensure that your design will fit perfectly within the piece of embroidery fabric you are using, it is necessary to find and mark the centre point. To do this, tack (baste) a row of stitches horizontally and vertically from the centre of each side of the fabric – these correspond to the arrows at the sides of each chart – where they meet is the centre point. You may like to stitch from the centre outwards or divide the design into sections, completing each one separately.

MAKING UP

When making up any item, a 1.5cm (5/8in) seam allowance has been used unless otherwise stated. Instructions for making up are included under each project, where appropriate. If making up a garment such as a waistcoat, mark out the pattern pieces on to the fabric before you start stitching to ensure each design is correctly placed. To prevent fabric from fraying, machine stitch around the edges or bind with tape.

USING THE CHARTS AND KEYS

All the designs in this book use DMC embroidery fabrics, stranded cotton (floss) or tapestry wool (yarn). The colours and symbols shown on the colour key correspond to DMC shade codes. Each project lists the number of skeins required for each colour code together with a colour name, which is given for easy reference only – when purchasing threads, use the correct shade code numbers. Each chart is in full colour, using colours that match the thread shades as closely as possible. Each coloured square on the chart has a symbol at the centre – these represent one complete cross stitch. The colours and symbols correspond to those listed in the key at the side of each chart. The number at the side of each box corresponds to the DMC shade code.

A quarter square represents a three-quarter cross stitch. French knots are indicated by a coloured square with a small white or black spot at the centre – the project instructions specify when they are used. A solid coloured line indicates backstitch. A solid straight line indicates long stitches for cats' whiskers and eyebrows - *note:* often shown in an easier-to-see colour on the charts.

Small black arrows at the sides of a chart indicate the centre and by lining these up you will find the centre point. Some of the larger charts are spread over four pages with the colour key repeated on each double page. To prevent mistakes, work systematically so that you read the chart accurately. Constantly check your progress against the chart and count the stitches as you go. If your eyesight is poor, you may find it helpful to enlarge the chart on a colour photocopier.

USING THE GRAPHS

Graphs are used to indicate where to place designs on the fabric and also to produce templates for making gifts and accessories, as in the Kittens Apron (see fig 6, page 43) and the Bean-Bag Bed (see fig 11, page 124). Each square on the graph represents 5cm (2in). Transfer the template onto ready-printed dressmaker's paper or draw your own graph paper. The templates have either a 6mm (¼in) or a 1.5cm (⅝in) seam allowance included – this is indicated in the project instructions.

MAKING BIAS BINDING

1 To make bias strips, fold over a corner of fabric at a 45 degree angle, then cut along the diagonal fold to give a bias edge. Use a pencil and ruler to mark out the diagonal lines on the fabric 5cm (2in) apart, then cut along the pencil lines to make the bias strips (see fig 1).

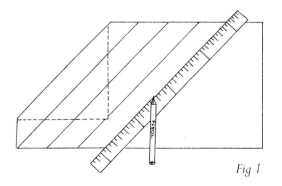

Fig 1

2 With right sides facing, place the bias strips at right angles so that the short diagonal edges meet. Stitch along these edges, then press the seam open. Repeat this process until your strip reaches the required length (see fig 2).

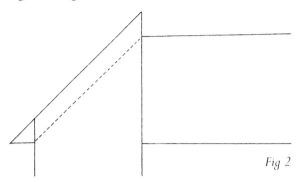

Fig 2

3 To make the binding, press a 1cm (½in) turning to the wrong side along each long edge, then bring the folds together, enclosing the raw edges and press. The binding is now ready to use.

USING WASTE CANVAS

Cross stitch is worked on various evenweave fabrics so that you can count the number of threads to work over, however, you may want to work a design on a textured fabric such as fleece or towelling and waste canvas has been specially designed to enable you to do this. It is available in a large variety of counts and is used just like Aida. It has blue lines running through it to mark off every five blocks making it easy to count your stitches. The waste canvas is tacked over your chosen fabric and is used as a temporary stitching surface which is then removed to leave the completed design on the fabric.

1 Cut a piece of waste canvas at least 5cm (2in) larger than your chosen design. Lay the canvas

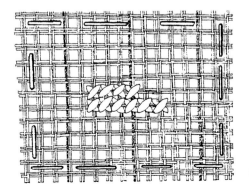

Fig 3

over your base fabric so that the blue lines run vertically along the grain of your fabric. Pin and tack (baste) the canvas in place (see fig 3), then work a row of tacking (basting) stitches vertically and horizontally across the canvas to mark the centre.

2 Stitch the design over the waste canvas following the project instructions for the cross stitch. When working, try to ensure that the corner of each stitch shares the hole with the previous stitch in the base fabric as this will give a neater finished effect.

3 When the stitching is complete, remove the tacking (basting) threads, using a pair of sharp scissors to trim away the excess waste canvas close to the cross stitches. Using a pair of tweezers carefully pull out the vertical threads of the waste canvas – the remaining horizontal threads can then be easily removed (see fig 4). If the waste canvas threads prove stubborn to remove it may help to slightly dampen them.

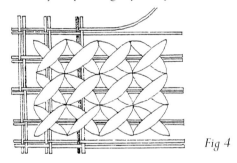

Fig 4

4 When all the waste canvas threads have been removed, press the design from the wrong side, then add any backstitches or French knots to complete your design.

WASHING AND PRESSING FINISHED WORK

If your work has become grubby during stitching, it can be gently hand washed in warm water using a soft liquid detergent. Use a soft nail brush to remove any stubborn marks, rinse in clean water, place the damp fabric on a clean white towel and leave to dry on a flat surface. Do not iron directly on to your work as this will flatten the stitches and spoil the finished effect. Lay the work face down on a clean, white towel, cover with a clean, fine cloth and then press.

MOUNTING AND FRAMING

It is best to take larger pictures to a professional framer, who will be able to stretch the fabric correctly and cut any surrounding mounts accurately. If mounting work into fire screens or footstools, follow the manufacturer's instructions. For smaller pieces, back with light-weight iron-on interfacing to prevent the fabric wrinkling, and then mount into plastic flexi-hoops, trinket boxes or cards, following the manufacturer's instructions.

TECHNIQUE TIPS

- Steam press the fabric before stitching to remove any stubborn creases.
- Mount fabric onto an embroidery frame to keep stitches smooth and flat.
- Work cross stitches with the top threads all facing in the same direction.
- Thread up lengths of several colours of stranded cotton (floss) into needles and arrange these at the side of your work by shade code number or by key reference.
- Work the designs from the centre outwards or split them into workable sections such as quarters. On larger designs, first work the main subject and then complete the background.
- When taking threads across the back of a design, weave the thread through the back of existing stitches to avoid any ugly lines showing through to the right side.
- Use short lengths of thread – about 30cm (12in) – to reduce any knotting and tangling.
- Check your work constantly against the chart to avoid making mistakes.
- For a smooth piece of work without any lumps or bumps, avoid using knots at the back of your work and cut off any excess threads as short as possible.
- Keep your work clean by packing it away in its own clean plastic bag to prevent any nasty accidents with spilt drinks, muddy paw prints or inquisitive fingers.

STITCH GUIDE

Cross stitch embroidery is a simple technique and the following diagrams show you how to work all the stitches used. Note that one block or thread refers to one block of Aida fabric or one thread of evenweave fabric.

STARTING AND FINISHING THREAD

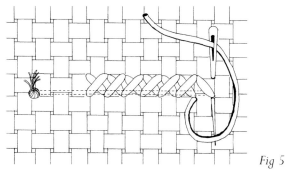

Fig 5

To start off your first length of thread, make a knot at one end and then push the needle through to the back of the fabric about 3cm (1¼in) from your starting point, leaving the knot on the right side. Stitch towards the knot, securing the thread at the back of the fabric as you go (see fig 5). When the thread is secure, cut off the knot. To finish off or start new threads, weave the thread into the back of worked stitches (see fig 6).

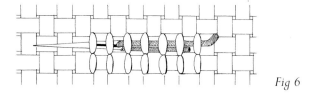

Fig 6

CROSS STITCH

Each coloured square on the chart represents one complete cross stitch which is worked in two easy stages.

Start by working one diagonal stitch over one block of Aida or two threads of linen, then work a second diagonal stitch over the first stitch, but in the opposite direction to form a cross (see fig 7). The cats in a row draught excluder on page 96 has been worked over two blocks

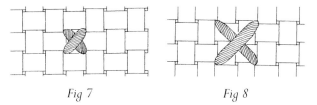

Fig 7   *Fig 8*

or four threads to produce a larger stitch (see fig 8). If you have a large area to cover, work a row of half stitches in one direction and work back in the opposite direction to complete each cross. The upper stitches should lie in the same direction to produce a neat effect (see fig 9).

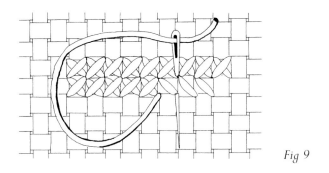

Fig 9

THREE-QUARTER CROSS STITCH

A small coloured square taking up a quarter of a square on the chart represents a three-quarter cross stitch.

To work this stitch, work the first half of the stitch in the normal way, then work the second diagonal stitch from the opposite corner but insert the needle at the centre of the cross, forming three-quarters of the complete stitch. A square showing two smaller coloured squares in opposite corners indicates that two of these stitches will have to be made back to back (see fig 10).

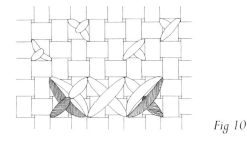

Fig 10

HALF CROSS STITCH

This stitch is used for the Wise Old Cat Doorstop on page 45, which is worked in tapestry wool (yarn). A half cross stitch is, simply, one half of a cross stitch, with the diagonal facing the same way as the upper stitches of each complete cross stitch (see fig 11).

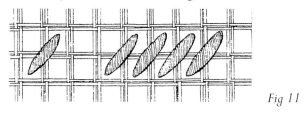

Fig 11

QUARTER CROSS STITCH

This is used for the Lion Wall Hanging, page 17, which is worked in half cross stitch using tapestry wool (yarn). When working a design on double mesh canvas using wool, a quarter cross stitch is used instead of a three-quarter cross stitch. So, where a three-quarter stitch is shown on the chart, use a quarter stitch instead.

To work a quarter cross stitch, start at one corner and work the quarter stitch in the same direction as the half stitches, but insert the needle at the centre of the square, therefore only forming a quarter of the complete stitch (see fig 12).

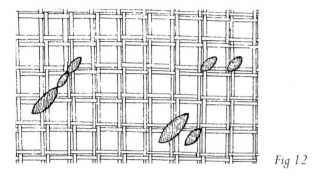

Fig 12

BACKSTITCH

Backstitch is indicated on the chart by a solid coloured line. It is worked around areas of completed cross stitches to add definition or on top of stitches to add detail.

To work backstitch start by pulling the needle through the hole in the fabric at 1, then push down through at 2. For the next stitch, pull the needle through at 3, push to the back at 1, then repeat the process to make the next stitch (see fig 13). This will give you short stitches at the front of your work and a longer stitch at the back. If working backstitch over two blocks or threads, such as when using linen, work each stitch over two threads (as for cross stitch in fig 8).

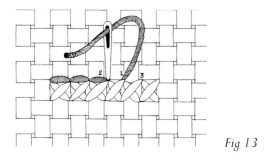

Fig 13

LONG STITCH

Long stitches are used to work whiskers and eyebrow hairs and are indicated on the chart by a straight, solid coloured line - often shown in a different, easier-to-see colour. Refer to the instructions for the actual colour. Work long stitches on top of the completed stitched design.

To work long stitch, pull the needle through the hole in the fabric at a point indicated on the chart, then push back through at the other end, to make a long stitch on top of the fabric. Repeat the process for the next stitch, carrying the thread across the back of the fabric to the next starting point (see fig 14).

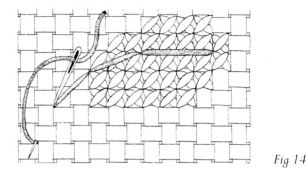

Fig 14

FRENCH KNOTS

These are small knots which are used to add detail, for example, the ladybird spots on the Cat-Nap Table Linen on page 50. They are indicated on the chart by a small white or black spot.

To work this stitch, bring the needle through to the front of the fabric and wind the thread tightly once around the needle. Hold the twisted thread firmly in place and carefully insert the needle one thread away from its starting position (see fig 15). For a larger knot, twist the thread two or three times around the needle.

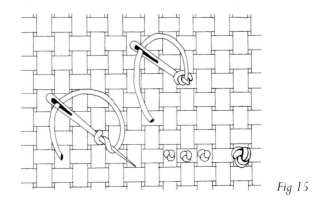

Fig 15

Lion Territory

This majestic lion is shown surveying his territory on the plains of Africa, ready to defend it and the lionesses and cubs that make up his pride. This stunning design is worked as a cushion in cross stitch, three-quarter cross stitch and backstitch using stranded cotton (floss). By using half cross stitches, the design has been modified to become an impressive wall hanging stitched in tapestry wool (yarn).

LIONS

Most big cats live solitary lives, but lions are social animals and live in small family groups or prides, sharing their territory with other members of the pride. Females always outnumber males in the pride, with close family members — sisters, daughters and aunts — staying together. Females do all the hunting, and by hunting together they are able to catch prey larger than themselves, like zebra and antelope. The males are always allowed to feed from the kill first. The role of male lions, distinguished by their full, thick manes around their head and neck, is to defend the pride and their territory. They do this by patrolling and marking their territory and by roaring, as a warning to others.

LION CUSHION

FINISHED DESIGN SIZE

34 x 36cm (13½ x 14¼in) approximately

WHAT YOU WILL NEED

- Desert Sand 28-count Cashel linen (E3281), 56cm (22in) square
- Lightweight iron-on interfacing 50cm (20in) square
- Cotton or linen fabric for backing, 30 x 90cm (³/₈yd x 36in) wide
- Thick furnishing braid, 2.3m (2½yd)
- Matching sewing thread
- Square cushion pad to fit

DMC STRANDED COTTON (FLOSS)

I skein: white; black 310; dark mahogany 300; med mahogany 301; dark khaki green 3011; med khaki green 3012; light khaki green 3013; dark yellow beige 3045; med yellow beige 3046; light yellow beige 3047; dark green grey 3051; black brown 3371; dark green grey 3768; light mahogany 3776; dark mahogany 400; light mahogany 402; dark hazelnut brown 420; light hazelnut brown 422; med golden brown 433; light golden brown 434; light tan 739; dark topaz 781; dark topaz 782; med topaz 783; dark coffee brown 801; dark hazelnut brown 869; med grey green 926; light grey green 927; light grey green 928; dark coffee brown 938; tawny 945

2 skeins: light golden brown 435; tan 436; light tan 437; light tan 738

1 Prepare your fabric for work, reading the Techniques section if necessary. Use a soft pencil to mark a 43cm (17in) square at the centre of the linen fabric. The design is worked at the centre of the square so mark the centre point.

2 To give a feeling of depth to the design, the lion is worked in cross stitch using two strands of stranded cotton (floss), while the background, foliage and sky areas use one strand. The backstitch and French knots also use one strand of stranded cotton (floss). Refer to the Stitch Guide on page 12 for how to work the stitches.

3 Work the backstitch detail using black 310 around the eye and black brown 3371 around the nose. Referring to the charts on pages 18–21 stitch grass heads and flower stems using one strand for backstitch and French knots in a mixture of dark khaki green 3011; med khaki green 3012; dark yellow beige 3045; med yellow beige 3046; light yellow beige 3047; dark hazelnut brown 420; light hazelnut brown 422 and dark hazelnut brown 869. Use one strand of white to work long stitches for the whiskers.

TO MAKE UP THE CUSHION

1 Following the manufacturer's instructions, iron the interfacing to the back of the embroidered fabric to strengthen it and secure the stitches. Cut away excess fabric along the marked pencil line, leaving an embroidered square with a 1.5cm (⅝in) seam allowance.

2 For the back, cut two pieces of cotton or linen 28 x 43cm (11 x 17in), and hem along one long edge on each. Lay the embroidered fabric face upwards on a flat surface. With right sides down, lay the two rectangles of the back over the front so that all raw edges match and hemmed edges overlap at the centre. Pin, tack (baste) and machine stitch the layers together along the stitching line. Turn through to the right side.

3 Add a braid edging to the cushion by cutting the furnishing braid into four equal lengths and hand stitching along each edge, leaving equal lengths extending at each end. Pinch together the two extensions at each corner, using matching sewing thread to tightly bind them together. Secure with a knot then fray the braid to make a tassel (see fig 1).

Fig 1   Making a tassel

LION WALL HANGING

FINISHED DESIGN SIZE
51 x 55cm (20 x 21³/₄ in) approximately

WHAT YOU WILL NEED
- Antique double thread canvas (E1231) 90cm (36in) square
- Large tapestry frame (optional)
- Tapestry needle
- Thimble
- Stick for hanging, 66cm (26in) long
- Flat braid, 40cm (16in)

DMC TAPESTRY WOOL (YARN), 8m (8³/₄yd) SKEINS
I skein: black 7310; dark mahogany 7459; med mahogany 7446; med khaki green 7424; light khaki green 7422; dark yellow beige 7423; med yellow beige 7493; light yellow beige 7501; dark green grey 7367; black brown 7419; dark green grey 7690; light mahogany 7176; dark mahogany 7178; light mahogany 7175; dark hazelnut brown 7525; light tan 7170; dark topaz 7783; dark topaz 7505; dark hazelnut brown 7514; med grey green 7927; light grey green 7692; dark coffee brown 7489; tawny 7171; med topaz 7078

2 skeins: white; dark khaki green 7376; light hazelnut brown 7511; med brown golden 7497; dark coffee brown 7479

3 skeins: light grey green 7587; light golden brown 7845

4 skeins: light tan 7460

5 skeins: light tan 7452; tan 7143; light golden brown 7059

6 skeins: light beige 7492

I I skeins: light blue 7301

1 Prepare your canvas, referring to the Techniques section if necessary. Canvas tends to stretch and lose its shape easily. To prevent this and make working easier, mount it on to a large frame and mark the centre point. When stitching use a large tapestry needle and a thimble to protect your fingers.

2 Refer to the Stitch Guide for how to work the stitches. Following the charts on pages 18–21 work the design using one strand of tapestry wool (yarn). Replace each whole cross stitch on the chart with a half cross stitch, and each three-quarter stitch with a quarter stitch (working on double mesh canvas will enable you to do this). Omit working any backstitch or French knots. Use one strand of wool (yarn) for the long stitches for the whiskers and eyebrows.

3 When the design is complete, trim away excess canvas to within 5cm (2in) of the stitches. Fold the canvas turnings to the back of the hanging, leaving two holes showing and one thread running across the top of the fold. Using sewing thread, stitch the turnings in place.

4 Finish the hanging by adding an overcast edging, using light blue 7301 to work the edging around the sky areas and light beige 7492 around the landscape and lion areas. Use two strands of tapestry wool (yarn), working one stitch in each hole to cover the canvas. Secure the thread at the back of the canvas, insert the needle into the hole nearest the cross stitches (or in this case, half cross stitches) and pull to the front of the canvas. The overcast thread should share a hole with the last stitch of the cross stitch design. Take the needle to the back of the canvas and work the next stitch in the same way (see fig 2).

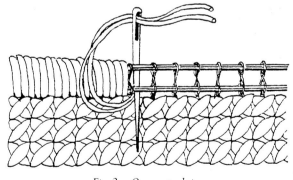

Fig 2   Overcast edging

5 Cut two 20cm (8in) strips of flat braid. Fold the strips in half to form a loop, then use sewing thread to hand stitch them in place at the back of the wall hanging at either end of the top edge. Finally, thread a stick through the loops and hang in place.

DMC tapestry wool (yarn)

▦ 7497	ꓧꓧ 7170	⊞ 7424	▦ 7178	⊞ 7514	⊡⊡ 7587
▦ 7479	7460	▦ 7376	▦ 7459	▦ 7367	⊡⊡ 7692
▦ 7489	ꓔꓔ 7452	√√ 7501	⟩⟩ 7078	‡‡ 7171	7927
▦ 7419	✛✛ 7143	7493	⋰⋰ 7505	⟋⟍ 7175	▼▼ 7690
∼∼ white	⊡⊡ 7059	7511	◤◥ 7783	7176	▦ 7525
⊡⊡ 7310	⊡⊡ 7845	7423	7422	⟍⟋ 7446	

18

DMC stranded cotton (floss)

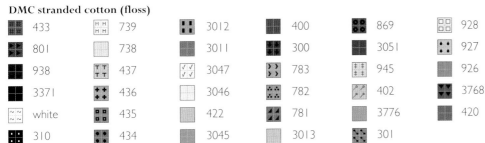

433	739	3012	400	869	928
801	738	3011	300	3051	927
938	437	3047	783	945	926
3371	436	3046	782	402	3776
white	435	422	781	3776	420
310	434	3045	3013	301	

DMC tapestry wool (yarn)

7497	7170	7424	7178	7514	7587
7479	7460	7376	7459	7367	7692
7489	7452	7501	7078	7171	7927
7419	7143	7493	7505	7175	7690
white	7059	7511	7783	7176	7525
7310	7845	7423	7422	7446	

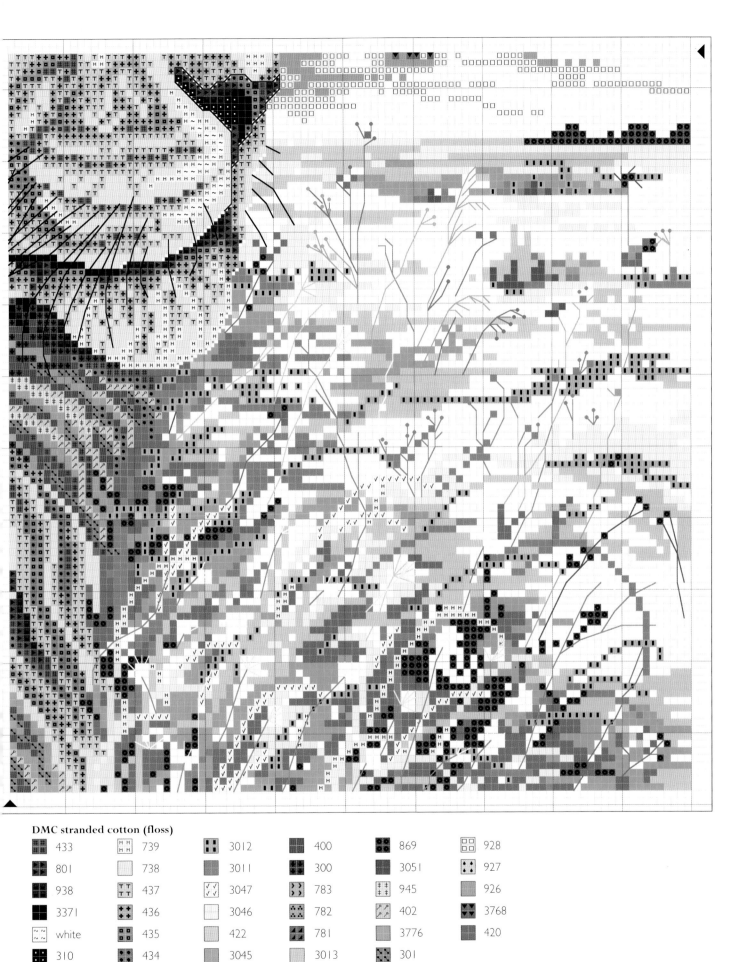

DMC stranded cotton (floss)

433	739	3012
801	738	3011
938	437	3047
3371	436	3046
white	435	422
310	434	3045

400	869	928
300	3051	927
783	945	926
782	402	3768
781	3776	420
3013	301	

Siamese Kitten and Butterfly

This design of a Siamese kitten shows the distinctive bright blue eyes, cream body and darker colouring of the face, ears, feet and tail. We have used the design for a variety of projects using a mixture of fabrics to show how versatile it is. The whole design is worked as a picture on 14-count Aida and also for a waistcoat on 28-count evenweave linen. The butterfly is used on its own for the teaspoon and jam pot cover.

SIAMESE KITTEN PICTURE

FINISHED DESIGN SIZE

13 x 17cm (5 x 6³/₄in) square approximately

WHAT YOU WILL NEED

• Platinum 14-count Aida, 33cm (13in) square

DMC STRANDED COTTON (FLOSS)

I skein: white; black 310; light peach 353; light golden brown 434; tan 436; med shell grey 452; light shell grey 453; avocado green 469; light tan 738; light tan 739; med tangerine 741; dark delft blue 798; med delft blue 799; dark coffee brown 801; dark hazelnut brown 869; med avocado green 937; dark coffee brown 938

1 Prepare your fabric for work, reading the Techniques section if necessary and marking the centre point. Refer to the Stitch Guide on page 12 for working the stitches and follow the chart on page 26. The picture is shown opposite.

2 Use two strands of stranded cotton (floss) for the cross stitch. Work backstitch using one strand of stranded cotton (floss) in black 310 around the cat's eyes, nose, mouth, and dark hazelnut brown 869 around the butterfly body and wings. Use one strand of white to work the long stitches for the whiskers.

3 Refer to Mounting and Framing on page 11 for how to complete your picture.

SIAMESE

The Siamese is one of the oldest and most popular of pedigree breeds and is the most recognisable. They have distinctive cream and chocolate colouring, a long slender body and limbs, with a long, wedge-shaped face and large, pointed ears. The large eyes are a brilliant deep blue and slightly slanted. If you choose this cat as a pet be prepared to give it plenty of attention and loving devotion. They are the most vocal of domestic cats and can be outgoing, excitable and hyperactive.

BUTTERFLY TEASPOON

The delightful Siamese Kitten Picture

FINISHED DESIGN SIZE

1cm (¹/₂in) square approximately

WHAT YOU WILL NEED

• Scrap of black 28-count evenweave linen
• Teaspoon for embroidery (available from Framecraft
  – see Stockists page 127)

DMC STRANDED COTTON (FLOSS)

Use the thread list for the Butterfly Jam Pot Cover page 25

1 Read the Techniques section beginning on page 9 if necessary and refer to the Stitch Guide on page 12 for how to work the stitches. Follow the butterfly chart on page 26 (and see photograph on page 25), using one strand of stranded cotton (floss) for the cross stitch and backstitch. Work backstitch in black 310 around the butterfly body and the dividing line between the wings.

2 To complete your teaspoon, follow the manufacturer's instructions.

SIAMESE KITTEN AND BUTTERFLY WAISTCOAT

FINISHED DESIGN SIZE

Kitten 13.5cm (5¼in) square approximately

Butterfly 2.5cm (1in) square approximately

WHAT YOU WILL NEED

- Purchased pattern for a waistcoat
- Biscuit 28-count Cashel linen (E3281), or other evenweave fabric (refer to pattern for requirements)
- Fabric for backing and lining (refer to pattern for fabric requirements)
- Buttons (refer to pattern for number required)
- Matching sewing thread

DMC STRANDED COTTON (FLOSS)

Use the thread list for the Siamese Kitten Picture on page 22

1 Lay the pattern pieces for the waistcoat fronts on the fabric and tack (baste) around the shapes with sewing thread. It may be easier to stitch the designs on to the linen fabric before cutting out the fronts.

2 Prepare your embroidery fabric, reading through the Techniques section if necessary. Refer to the Stitch Guide on page 12 for how to work the stitches. The Siamese kitten is stitched on one waistcoat front and the butterfly motif is stitched randomly over the other front.

3 Follow the chart on page 26, using two strands of stranded cotton (floss) for the cross stitch and one strand for the backstitch, worked over two threads of evenweave fabric. Work the backstitch detail in black 310 around the cat's eyes, nose and mouth and around each butterfly body and wings. Use one strand of white to work the long stitches for the cat's whiskers.

4 Make up the waistcoat following the instructions for the purchased paper pattern. Finish by adding buttons which complement the colours of the design, or add covered fabric buttons.

BUTTERFLY JAM POT COVER

FINISHED DESIGN SIZE

4cm (1¾in) square approximately

WHAT YOU WILL NEED

- Jam pot cover for embroidery with 18-count central Aida section (available from Framecraft — see Stockists page 127)

DMC STRANDED COTTON (FLOSS)

I skein: white; black 310; light shell grey 453; med shell grey 452; med tangerine 741; dark hazelnut brown 869

1 Read the Techniques section if necessary and refer to the Stitch Guide for how to work the stitches.

2 Follow the butterfly chart on page 26 (and see photograph below). Use three strands of stranded cotton (floss) for the cross stitch and one strand for the backstitch, worked over two blocks of Aida. Work backstitch in black 310 around the butterfly body and to outline the wings and your cover is ready.

Siamese Kitten and Butterfly

DMC stranded cotton (floss)

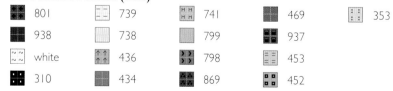

	801		739		741		469		353
	938		738		799		937		
	white		436		798		453		
	310		434		869		452		

Sitting Pretty

*T*his ambitious design captures the cosy image of a contented marmalade cat, draped lazily over a floral chintz armchair. A combination of cross stitch, three-quarter cross stitch and backstitch help to create the stunning detail of this wonderful cat worked on white 14-count Aida. A feeling of depth is created in the finished picture by working the background areas using only one strand of thread in the needle.

FINISHED DESIGN SIZE

35 x 37cm (13³/₄ x 14¹/₂in) approximately

WHAT YOU WILL NEED

• White 14-count Aida 51cm (20in) square

DMC STRANDED COTTON (FLOSS)

I skein: white; black 310; dark shell pink 221; light shell pink 223; light shell pink 224; light shell pink 225; dark mahogany 300; med khaki green 3012; light khaki green 3013; med silver plum 3041; light silver plum 3042; dark yellow beige 3045; med yellow beige 3046; light yellow beige 3047; dark pine green 3362; med pine green 3363; pine green 3364; black brown 3371; peach 351; light peach 352; light peach 353; dark desert sand 3722; light silver plum 3743; light tawny 3770; light yellow 3823; dark rust 3826; light rust 3827; dark golden sand 3829; dark hazelnut brown 420; light beige brown 543; dark drab brown 611; med drab brown 612; light drab brown 613; light golden sand 676; med golden sand 729; light yellow 745; dark coffee brown 801; med beige brown 840; light beige brown 841; light beige brown 842; black avocado green 934; dark coffee brown 938; tawny 945; light tawny 951; dark rust 975; med rust 976; light rust 977

CATS AND SLEEP

Cats sleep much longer than other mammals, usually for sixteen hours a day or even longer in hot countries. Most sleeping is done during the day so they are awake in the early morning and late evening, when it's cooler and hunting is more productive. Rather than having long deep sleeps they prefer cat-naps — a drowsy light sleep, usually with one eye slightly open, from which they are easily roused. After about thirty minutes, they enter six minutes of deep dream sleep then return to drowsing. This is followed by a waking ritual of yawning, stretching and washing, to exercise their muscles, revive circulation, and restore body scent. Cats usually sleep in the best chair in the house or on the bed because they recognise the smell and feel safe, but if a cat starts to sleep on your bed, it will expect to sleep there for the rest of its life!

1 Prepare your fabric for work, reading the Techniques section if necessary and marking the centre point. Refer to the Stitch Guide for how to work the stitches.

2 Following the charts on pages 30–33 work the cat and foreground first, then complete the background. The cat and the front arm of the armchair are worked in cross stitch using two strands of stranded cotton (floss). The background area that includes everything behind the cat, is worked in cross stitch using one strand of stranded cotton (floss).

3 Backstitch is worked using one strand of stranded cotton (floss). Work backstitch detail using black 310 around the eyes, dark coffee brown 801 around the mouth and nose, and golden brown 3826 around the ears. Work long continuous backstitches using one strand of white for the whiskers and eyebrows.

4 Refer to Mounting and Framing on page 11 for how to complete your picture.

CAT TERRITORY

Cats make wonderful companions but they do need their independence and like to come and go as they please. They are most active during the early morning and late evening, usually when we are asleep, and one of their favourite activities is to patrol and defend their territory which usually consists of their owner's garden walls and fences. Their home is the most important part of their territory, as it provides them with regular food, a safe place to rest, and, with the help of a cat flap, is always accessible.

DMC stranded cotton (floss)

3827	801	840	3829	3363	3722	745	611
945	300	841	729	3364	223	3823	612
951	975	842	676	420	224	3041	613
3770	3826	543	351	3045	225	3042	3012
white	976	3371	352	3046	934	3743	3013
310	977	938	353	3047	3362	221	

30

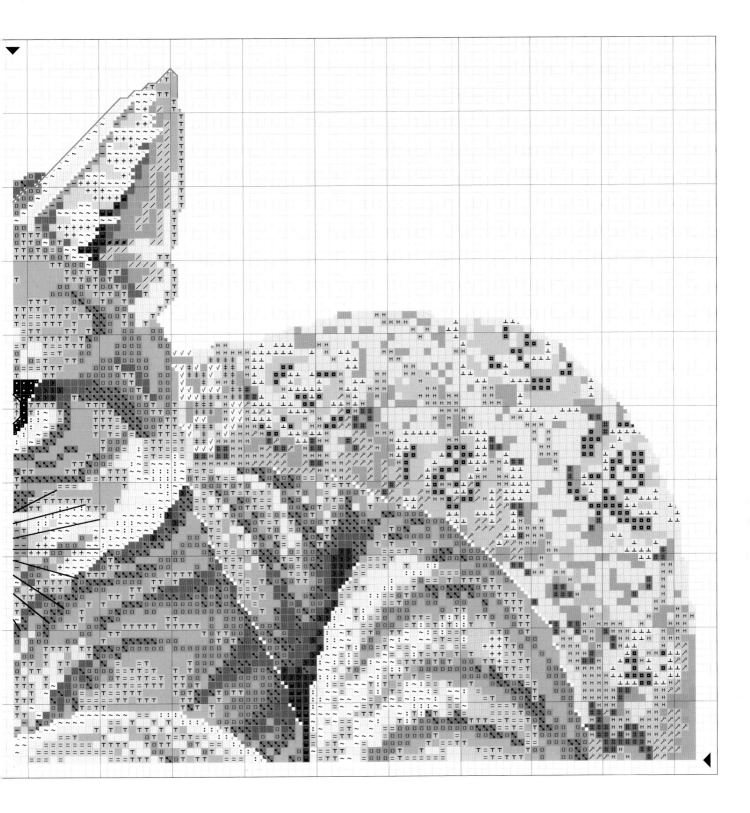

DMC stranded cotton (floss)

3827	801	840	3829
945	300	841	729
951	975	842	676
3770	3826	543	351
white	976	3371	352
310	977	938	353

3363	3722	745	611
3364	223	3823	612
420	224	3041	613
3045	225	3042	3012
3046	934	3743	3013
3047	3362	221	

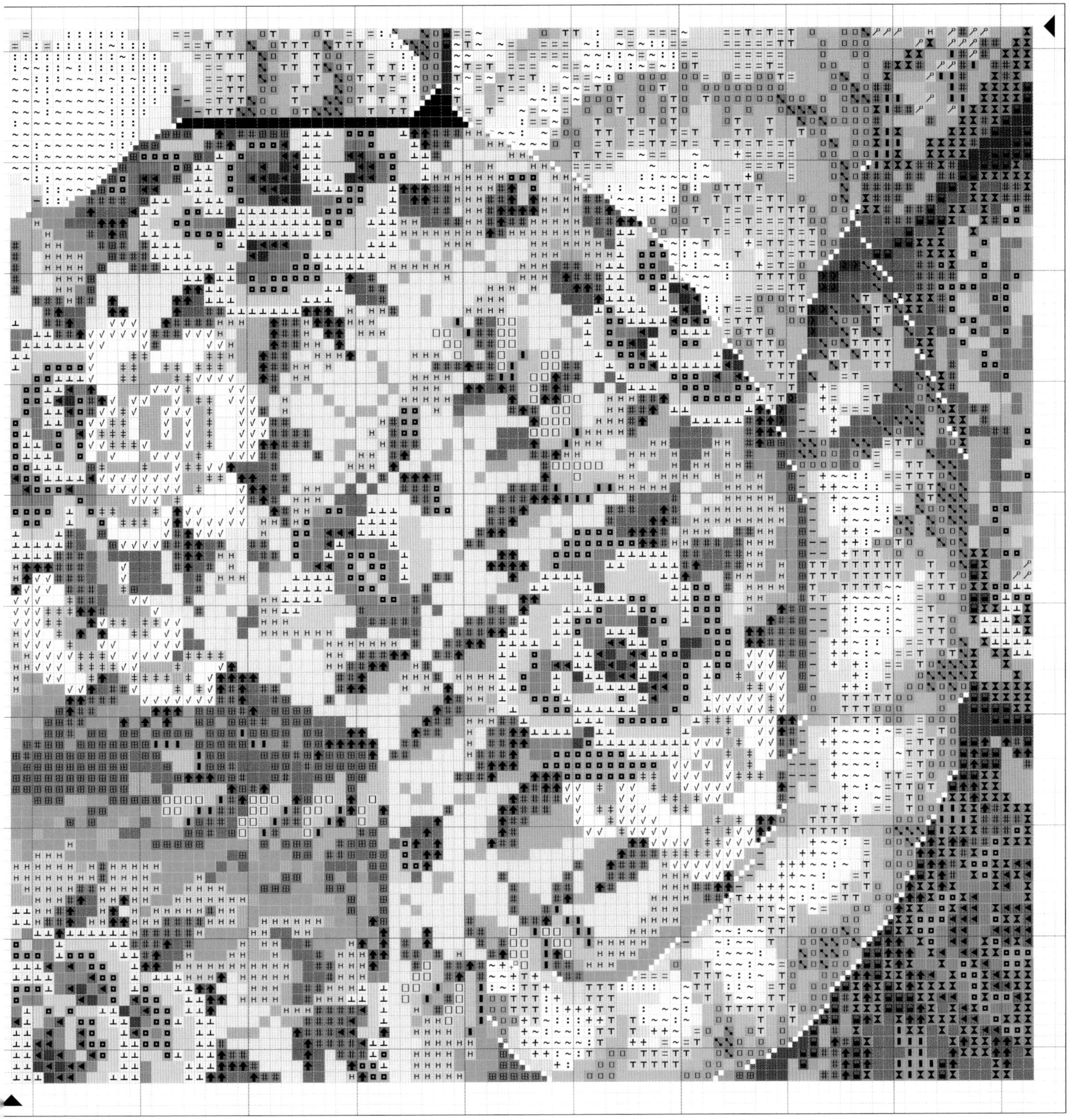

Serval Fire Screen

This magnificent fire screen design shows an alert serval cat amongst the foliage of the African grassland plains. This distinctive member of the big cat family has a spotted coat, dark-tipped ringed tail and very large ears. The design is worked in cross stitch and three-quarter cross stitch, with long stitches to add the whisker detail. The orange and rust shades of the fur and the green foliage are complemented beautifully by the khaki Aida, but the design would look equally as stunning on a black background.

THE SERVAL CAT

Serval are widespread and can be found in the grass-lands and plains throughout Africa and Western Asia. They are one of the most striking of the savannah cats, with their small head, distinctive spotted coat, ringed tail and long legs, they look like a small cheetah. Plains cats are mostly nocturnal and have longer legs than other cats enabling them to run at fast speeds over short distances to escape from larger predators like hyenas. Serval like to live near water and hunt small animals like rodents, lizards, beetles, and snakes and they often climb trees to catch birds. They have been hunted both for meat and for their fur which is used for the traditional cloaks worn by East Africans.

FINISHED DESIGN SIZE
25 x 36cm (9³/₄ x 14¹/₄ in) approximately

WHAT YOU WILL NEED
- Khaki 14-count Aida, 56 x 68cm (22 x 27in)
- Fire screen for embroidery (see Stockists page 127)

DMC STRANDED COTTON (FLOSS)
I skein: white; black 310; silver grey 317; med pine green 3363; med desert sand 3773; dark silver grey 413; avocado green 469; light avocado green 470; light avocado green 471; light avocado green 472; fern green 522; light fern green 523; dark beige grey 642; med beige grey 644; light golden sand 676; light golden sand 677; dark golden sand 680; med golden sand 729; off white 746; dark topaz 782; med topaz 783; dark beige brown 838; dark beige brown 839; dark hazelnut brown 869; dark avocado green 936; light desert sand 950

1 Prepare your fabric for work, reading the Techniques section if necessary and marking the centre point. Refer to the Stitch Guide on page 12 for how to work the stitches.

2 When stitching the design use two strands of stranded cotton (floss) for the cross stitch. Work the long stitches last, using one strand of white for the whiskers and eyebrows.

3 To mount the completed embroidery into the fire screen, follow the manufacturer's instructions.

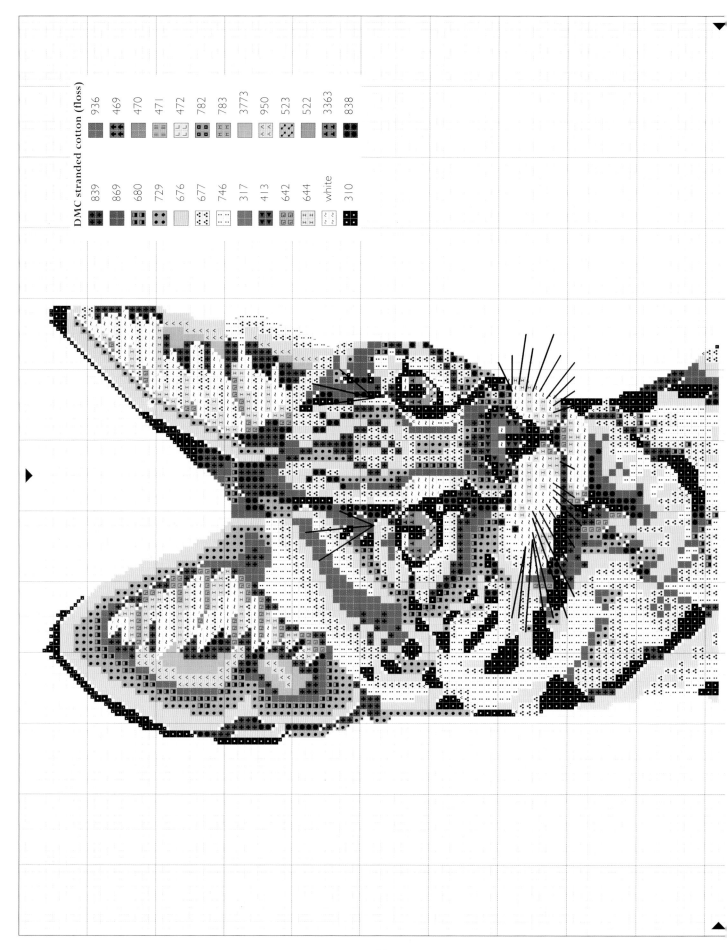

DMC stranded cotton (floss)

	936		839
	469		869
	470		680
	471		729
	472		676
	782		677
	783		746
	3773		317
	950		413
	523		642
	522		644
	3363		white
	838		310

Kittens Breakfast Set

This delightful collection of kitten designs is used to decorate a breakfast set of egg cosies, placemats, cafétière cover and apron. The designs use a variety of cross stitch, three-quarter cross stitch, backstitch and long stitches, worked up on Aida. The egg cosies use the design for the black and white kitten with the stitched ears replaced by fabric ears which are sewn on when the cross stitching is complete.

DMC STRANDED COTTON (FLOSS)

British Blue Kitten

I skein: white; black 310; silver grey 317; light silver grey 318; dark pewter grey 3799; dark rust 3826; dark silver grey 413; dark silver grey 414; moss green 581; med rust 976

Work the backstitch detail using one strand of black 310 around the eyes and nose. Work the long stitches using one strand of light silver grey 318 for the whiskers and eyebrows

Ginger Tabby Kitten

I skein: white; black 310; light peach 352; light peach 353; light tawny 3770; light moss green 3819; dark rust 3826; light rust 3827; moss green 581; med beige brown 840; light beige brown 841; light beige brown 842; tawny 945; light tawny 951; dark rust 975; med rust 976; light rust 977

Work the backstitch detail using one strand of black 310 around the eyes, and med beige brown 840 around the nose. Work the long stitches using one strand of white for the whiskers and eyebrows

Black and White Kitten

I skein: white; black 310; light beaver grey 3072; silver grey 317; light silver grey 318; light peach 352; light peach 353; dark pewter grey 3799; dark silver grey 413; dark silver grey 414; dark beaver grey 646; med beaver grey 647; light beaver grey 648; light blue 813; dark blue 825; med blue 826

KITTENS PLACEMATS

FINISHED DESIGN SIZE

9 x 20.5cm (3½ x 8in) approximately

WHAT YOU WILL NEED (for each placemat)

- Cream 14-count Aida, 23 x 33cm (9 x 13in)
- Contrast cotton fabric, 30 x 90cm (³⁄₈yd x 36in) wide
- Medium-weight polyester wadding (batting), 28 x 42cm (11 x 16½in)
- Contrast bias binding, 1.6m (1¾yd)
- Matching sewing thread
- Ric-rac braid, 90cm (1yd)

DMC STRANDED COTTON (FLOSS)

Use the thread list for the British Blue and Ginger Tabby

1 Read through Techniques and prepare your fabric, marking the centre point. Refer to the Stitch Guide on page 12 for working the stitches.

2 Stitch the two kittens following the charts on page 42. Use two strands of stranded cotton (floss) for the cross stitch and one strand for the backstitch and long stitches, referring to the thread lists for the details.

TO MAKE EACH PLACEMAT

1 For each placemat cut two 28 x 42cm (11 x 16½in) rectangles from cotton fabric and one from wadding (batting). Trim away excess Aida fabric from the completed design to leave a patch 15 x 26cm (6 x 10¼in).

2 For the placemat front, pin and tack (baste) the embroidered patch centrally to the right side of one cotton rectangle. Machine stitch the patch in place, making a row of stitches 1cm (½in) from the outer edges, then stitch ric-rac braid over the machine stitches to make a border. Finish the patch with a frayed edging, made by teasing out the threads at the outer edges.

3 Lay the remaining cotton shape right side down on a flat surface. Place the wadding (batting) on top, then lay the placemat front, right side up, on top so that the wadding (batting) is sandwiched between the two fabric layers. Pin and tack (baste) the fabric and wadding layers together.

4 To finish, bind around the straight edges of the placemat with a ready-made decorative bias binding or make your own (see Making Bias Binding page 10). To attach the bias binding, open out the folded edges, lay the binding along the edge to be bound so that right sides are facing and all the raw edges match. Pin, tack (baste) and stitch along the fold line, taking a 1cm (½in) seam allowance. Turn the binding down and over to the wrong side to form an edging. Fold in the raw edge of the binding so that it covers the line of machine stitches and hand stitch in place along the folded edge (see fig 3).

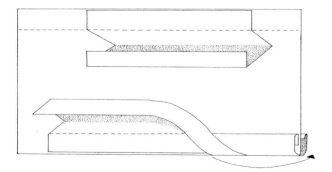

Fig 3   Attaching bias binding

KITTEN EGG COSIES

FINISHED DESIGN SIZE

9cm (3½in) square approximately

WHAT YOU WILL NEED (for each egg cosy)

- White 14-count Aida, 23cm (9in) square
- Scraps of black washable felt for ears and backing
- Scraps of lightweight polyester wadding (batting)
- Scraps of lining fabric
- Contrast bias binding 25cm (¼yd)
- Matching sewing thread

DMC STRANDED COTTON (FLOSS)

Use the thread list for the Black and White Kitten on page 38

1 Follow steps 1 and 2 for the Kittens Placemats on page 38 but use the chart for the black and white kitten on page 43.

TO MAKE THE EGG COSIES

1 Cut around the embroidered shape leaving 6mm (¼in) around the curved edges and 2cm (¾in) along the bottom edge. Use this shape as a template to cut one shape from backing fabric and two shapes each from polyester wadding (batting) and lining fabric for each egg cosy.

2 With right sides down, lay the lining shapes side by side on a flat surface. Place one wadding (batting) shape on top of each lining shape. Then, with right sides up, place the embroidered Aida and the felt backing shapes, one on top of each wadding (batting) shape, sandwiching the wadding between the two fabric layers. Tack (baste) these fabric and wadding pieces together in this way to form the front and back pieces of the egg cosy.

3 Trace the pattern for the ears from the fig 4 template. Cut two ear shapes from black felt, fold each shape along the marked line then tack (baste) the fold in place.

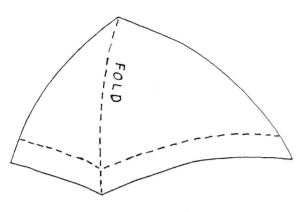

Fig 4   Ear template

4 To attach the ears, place them over the embroidered Aida with right sides facing so the bottom edge of each ear shape matches the top edges of the embroidered kitten's head (see fig 5). Pin and tack (baste) in place.

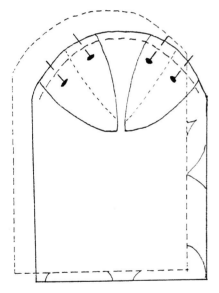

Fig 5   Attaching ears to the egg cosy

5 Bind the bottom straight edge of each egg cosy shape with a ready-made decorative bias binding or make your own (see Making Bias Binding page 10). To attach the binding, follow step 4 on page 40.

6 With right sides facing, place the front and back shapes together so that the ears are inside. Pin, tack (baste) and machine stitch round the outer curved edges as close to the embroidered stitching as possible. Finally, turn the egg cosy right side out and the ears will stick up.

KITTENS

A pregnant cat will find a secluded warm place where she can give birth to her litter. The new-born are blind and deaf and the helpless kittens rely on their mother to provide them with food, warmth and to protect them from predators. Although born deaf and blind they have an acute sense of smell which helps them find their way to the mother's teats to suckle milk as soon as they are born. The new-born kittens develop rapidly: by a week old their birth weight has doubled, at ten days their eyes open, at three weeks they begin to investigate their surroundings and at four weeks they have a complete set of baby teeth and begin to tear at tiny pieces of meat. Kittens rapidly develop into playful bundles of fun, ready to leave their mother and siblings at about twelve weeks old and enter the independent world.

Kittens Breakfast Set

DMC stranded cotton (floss)
Ginger Tabby

	352
o o	353
	3819
▢▢	581
◄◄	840
	841
↑↑	842
••	975
▫▫	3826
	976
H H	977
	3827
√√	945
L L	951
: :	3770
~ ~	white
▪▪	310

DMC stranded cotton (floss)
British Blue

↑↑	318
	414
▪▪	317
	413
▨▨	3799
▢▢	581
	976
▫▫	3826
~ ~	white
▪▪	310

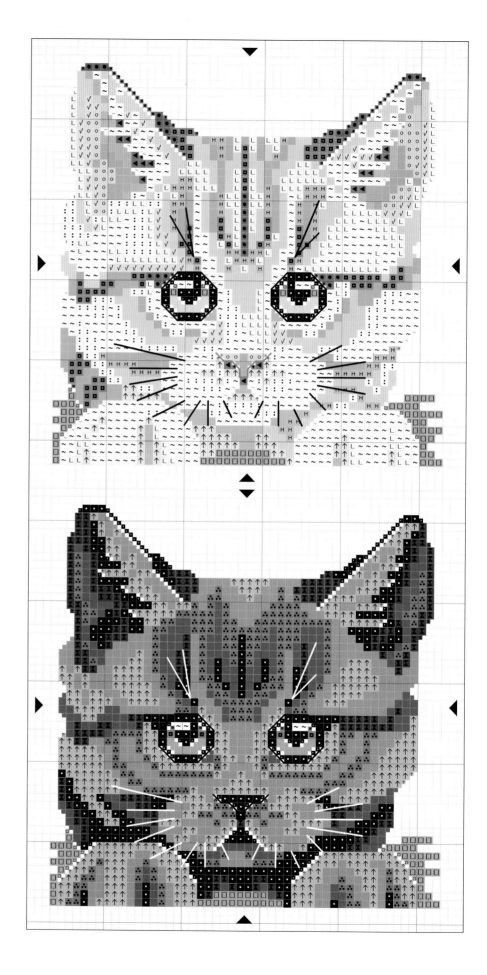

42

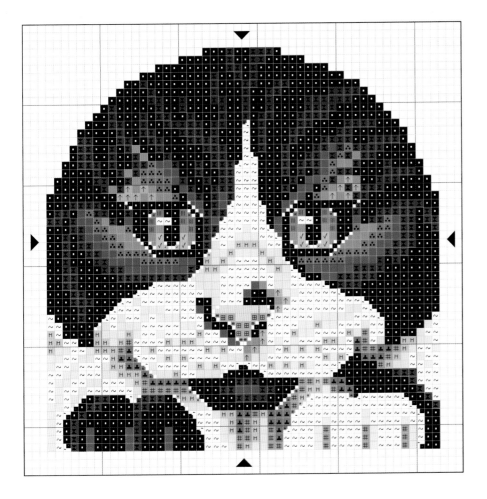

DMC stranded cotton (floss)
Black and White Kitten

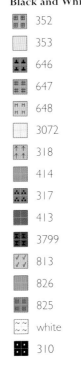

⊞⊞	352
	353
▲▲	646
♯♯	647
H H	648
	3072
↑↑	318
	414
∴∴	317
	413
✕✕	3799
✓✓	813
	826
⊞⊞	825
~ ~	white
■■	310

KITTENS APRON

FINISHED DESIGN SIZE

Each design is 9cm (3½in) square approximately

WHAT YOU WILL NEED

- Cream 14-count Aida, two pieces 18cm (7in) square, and one piece 21cm (8¼in) square
- Novelty print cotton fabric, 70 x 90cm (¾yd x 36in) wide
- Cream cotton webbing, 1.80m (2yd)
- Scraps of washable felt for the ears
- Contrast bias binding, 1.10m (1¼yd)
- Ric-rac braid, 1.8m (2yd)
- Matching sewing thread

DMC STRANDED COTTON (FLOSS)

Use the thread lists for the British Blue, Ginger Tabby and Black and White kittens on page 38

1 Follow steps 1 and 2 for the Kittens Placemats on page 38.

TO MAKE THE APRON

1 Use the graph to draw out a template of the apron pattern (see fig 6), referring to Using the Graphs page 10 for instructions.

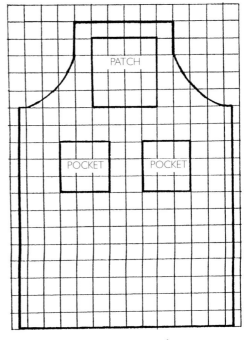

Fig 6   Apron template

2 Cut one apron shape from the cotton print fabric. From the cotton webbing, cut one 56cm (22in) strip for the neck band and two 60cm (23¹/₂in) strips for the waist ties.

3 Stitch the ginger tabby and British blue kittens in the centres of the 18cm (7in) squares of Aida (these will become the apron pockets) and the black and white kitten in the centre of the 21cm (8¹/₄in) square of Aida, following the charts on pages 42 and 43.

4 To make the fabric ears for the black and white kitten, trace the ear template (fig 4 page 41) omitting the 6mm (¹/₄in) seam allowance along the bottom edge. Cut two ear shapes from black felt and fold each ear along the marked line. Position the ears at either side of the embroidered kitten head and pin, tack (baste) and stitch in place.

5 Pin and tack (baste) the black and white kitten patch centrally to the front of the apron (see photograph page 39). Machine stitch the patch in place, making a row of stitches 1cm (¹/₂in) from the outer edges, then stitch ric-rac braid over the machine stitches to make a border. Finish the patch with a frayed edging by teasing out the threads at the outer edges.

6 Bind the top edge of each embroidered pocket shape with a ready-made decorative bias binding or you could make your own binding (see Making Bias Binding page 10). To attach the binding, follow step 4 on page 40 of the making up instructions for the Kittens Placemats.

7 Press a 1.5cm (⁵/₈in) hem along the remaining pocket edges. Pin, tack (baste) and machine stitch the pockets to the apron front, then stitch ric-rac braid around the pocket edges for decoration.

8 To complete the apron, machine stitch a 1.5cm (⁵/₈in) hem along the straight top, side and bottom edges. Stitch bias binding along the curved side edges, then stitch the neck band ends to the top corners and the ties to the apron sides.

KITTENS CAFETIERE COVER

FINISHED DESIGN SIZE
9 x 20.5cm (3¹/₂ x 8in) approximately

WHAT YOU WILL NEED
- Cream 14-count Aida, 15 x 35cm (6 x 14in)
- Contrast cotton backing fabric, 15 x 35cm (6 x 14in)
- Medium-weight polyester wadding (batting), 15 x 35cm (6 x 14in)
- Contrast bias binding, 1.10m (1¹/₄yd)
- Ric-rac braid, 90cm (1yd)
- Ribbon for ties, 40cm (¹/₂yd)
- Matching sewing thread

DMC STRANDED COTTON (FLOSS)
Use the thread list for the British Blue and Ginger Tabby kittens on page 38

1 Read through Techniques if necessary and prepare your fabric, marking the centre point. Refer to the Stitch Guide for working the stitches.

2 Fold the Aida in half, then stitch a kitten in the centre of each half (charts on page 42). Use two strands of stranded cotton (floss) for the cross stitch and one for the backstitch and long stitches. Refer to the thread lists on page 38 for the backstitch details.

3 Lay the cotton backing right side down on a flat surface. Place the wadding (batting) shape on top then the embroidered Aida on top, right side up, so that the wadding is sandwiched between the two fabrics. Pin and tack (baste) the fabric and wadding layers together.

4 Bind around the straight edges of the cafetière cover with a ready-made decorative bias binding or make your own (see Making Bias Binding page 10). To attach the bias binding follow step 4 on page 40.

5 Stitch ric-rac braid around the edge of the design, then stitch a ribbon tie 3.5cm (1¹/₂in) down from each corner along each short edge to finish.

Wise Old Cat

This delightful design, made into a tea-cosy and doorstop, shows a 'wise old cat' perched on a book. Our tea-cosy is cross stitched in silk threads on green Aida. It is also worked in wool for a shaped doorstop. You could also make a cushion filled with polyester filling.

WISE OLD CAT DOORSTOP

FINISHED DESIGN SIZE
33 x 46cm (13 x 18in)
approximately

WHAT YOU WILL NEED
- Antique 10-count double-thread canvas (E1231), 60 x 70cm (24 x 28in)
- Heavyweight cotton backing fabric, 50 x 60cm (20 x 24in)
- Medium-weight iron-on interfacing, 50 x 60cm (20 x 24in)
- Polyester wadding (batting) for filling
- Matching sewing thread
- Kitty litter or sawdust for filling
- An old sock

DMC TAPESTRY WOOL (YARN), 8m (8³/₄yd) SKEINS
1 skein: dark peach 7849; med peach 7106; light peach 7011; light peach 7762; light avocado green 7548; light avocado green 7549; light beige brown 7450; ecru; dark topaz 7767; med topaz 7783; dark coffee brown 7938; dark garnet 7110; dark coral red 7544; dark beige brown 7467; dark beige brown 7518; med beige brown 7519; light beige brown 7521; light beige brown 7520; med forest green 7042

2 skeins: white; black brown 7535; med golden brown 7479; light golden brown 7497; light golden brown 7845; light tan 7143; light tan 7452; light tan 7491

3 skeins: tan 7059; dark coffee brown 7469

4 skeins: black 7310

5 skeins: dark navy blue 7307

1 Prepare your canvas in the same way as for an evenweave fabric, reading through the Techniques section and marking the centre point. Canvas tends to lose its shape easily. To prevent this and make working easier, mount on to a large embroidery frame.

2 Work the design from the centre outwards, using a large tapestry needle and a thimble to protect your fingers. Follow the chart on page 48 and use one strand of tapestry wool (yarn) for the half cross stitch.

3 When the main design is complete, use a pencil to draw a line around the design, about 3cm (1¹/₄in) from the worked stitches – this is for the background area which is filled in with stitches using dark navy blue 7307.

TO MAKE THE DOORSTOP

1 Back the completed design with medium-weight iron-on interfacing (see manufacturer's instructions). Use a soft pencil to draw a line all around the design 1.5cm (⁵/₈in) from the finished embroidery and cut away excess fabric along this line. Cut a piece of cotton backing fabric to the same shape.

2 With right sides facing, place the front and back pieces together then pin and tack (baste) around the edges. Machine stitch the layers together, taking a 1.5cm (⁵/₈in) seam allowance and leaving a 20cm (8in) gap along the bottom straight edge for turning.

3 Turn the doorstop through to the right side and almost fill with wadding (batting). Next, fill the sock with kitty litter or sawdust and tie a knot at the end. Insert the filled sock into the base of the doorstop then secure the gap with slipstitches.

WISE OLD CAT TEA-COSY

FINISHED DESIGN SIZE

26 x 35cm (10¼ x 13¾in) approximately

WHAT YOU WILL NEED

- Christmas Green 14-count Aida, 40 x 50cm (16 x 20in)
- Cotton backing fabric, 40 x 50cm (16 x 20in)
- Medium-weight polyester wadding (batting), 40 x 90cm (½yd x 36in) wide
- Lining fabric, 40 x 90cm (½yd x 36in) wide
- Matching sewing thread

DMC STRANDED COTTON (FLOSS)

I skein: white; black brown 3371; dark peach 349; med peach 350; light peach 352; light peach 353; med golden brown 433; light golden brown 434; light golden brown 435; tan 436; light tan 437; light avocado green 471; light avocado green 472; light beige brown 543; cream 712; light tan 738; light tan 739; dark topaz 782; med topaz 783; dark coffee brown 801; dark garnet 814; dark coral red 817; dark beige brown 838; dark beige brown 839; med beige brown 840; light beige brown 841; light beige brown 842; dark coffee brown 938; med forest green 988

2 skeins: black 310

1 Prepare your fabric for work, reading through the Techniques section and Stitch Guide if necessary and marking the centre point. Follow the chart on pages 48 and 49 and use two strands of stranded cotton (floss) for the cross stitch.

TO MAKE THE TEA-COSY

1 Use the graph to draw out a template of the tea cosy pattern (see fig 7), referring to Using the Graphs page 10 for instructions. Place the template centrally over the stitched design, making sure that the bottom edge of the pattern is 3cm (1¼in) below the bottom embroidered edge of the cat. Cut one shape in Aida and one in cotton backing fabric. Cut two shapes each from wadding (batting) and lining fabric.

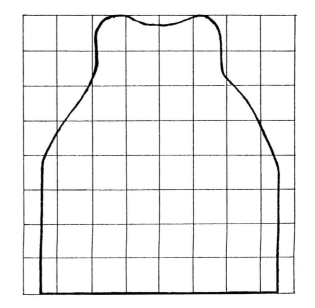

Fig 7   Tea-cosy template

2 Lay the wadding (batting) shapes flat side by side. With right sides up, place the embroidered Aida and the backing fabric one on top of each wadding (batting) shape. Tack (baste) the fabric and wadding (batting) together to form the front and back of the tea-cosy, working the stitches 1.5cm (⅝in) from the outer edges.

3 With right sides facing and wadding (batting) outwards, place the front and back pieces together. Pin, tack (baste) and machine stitch round the outer curved edges, using the tacking (basting) stitches as a guide. Trim away excess wadding (batting) to 6mm (¼in) from the seam line. Secure the wadding (batting) and fabric at the lower edges by tacking (basting) close to the straight edges. Turn the tea-cosy shape right side out, then turn up a 2.5cm (1in) hem along the bottom straight edge and tack (baste) in place.

4 Pin, tack (baste) and machine stitch the lining pieces together along the curved edges, then turn up a 3cm (1¼in) hem and press. Place the lining inside the tea-cosy shape, concealing all seam edges. Pin both layers together along the straight hemmed edges matching the side seams. Finish by slipstitching the two hemmed edges together.

DMC tapestry wool (yarn)

7783, 7767, 7106, 7849, 7544, 7110, 7042, 7548, 7549, 7467, 7518, 7519, 7521, 7520, 7450

7011, 7762, ecru, 7491, 7452, 7143, 7059, 7845, 7497, 7479, 7938, 7469, 7535, white, 7310

DMC stranded cotton (floss)

352, 353, 712, 739, 738, 817, 814, 988, 471, 472, 838, 839, 840, 841, 842, 543

783, 782, 350, 349, 437, 436, 435, 434, 433, 801, 938, 3371, white, 310

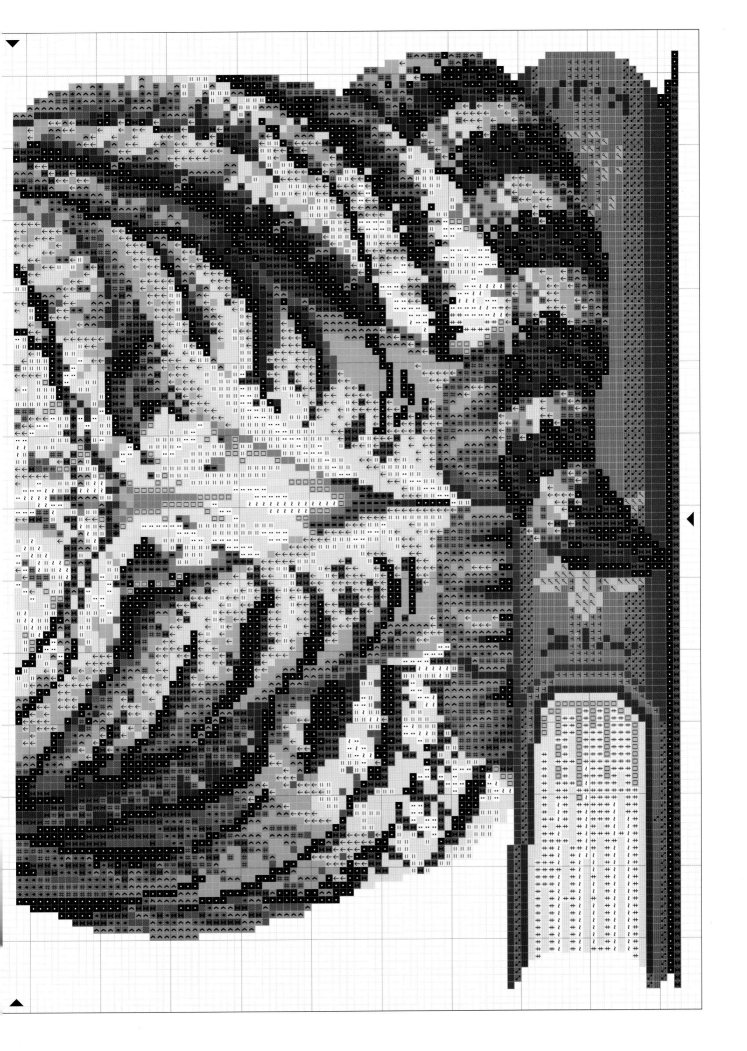

CAT-NAP TABLE LINEN

*D*uring lazy summer days in the garden, cats seem to doze all day long in shady spots or amongst pretty flower beds. This charming design shows a contented ginger tom snoozing in a bed of orange and yellow nasturtiums with delicate butterflies fluttering overhead, and, if you look closely, you can also see a tiny ladybird. The design has been worked on 28-count evenweave linen to make a stunning tablecloth, with elements of the design worked on a mixture of linen and Aida for matching napkins and a tray.

CAT-NAP TABLECLOTH

FINISHED DESIGN SIZES
Large floral garland
20.5 x 20.5 x 29cm (8 x 8 x 11½in)

Common blue butterfly
3 x 2.5cm (1⅛ x 1in)

Large white butterfly
3.5cm (1½in) square

Small tortoiseshell butterfly
5 x 5.5cm (2 x 2¼in)

WHAT YOU WILL NEED
• Cream 28-count Brittney (E3270) or other linen or evenweave fabric, 1.10m (1¼yd) square
• Matching sewing thread

DMC STRANDED COTTON (FLOSS)
1 skein: black 310; white; med mocha brown 3032; light mocha brown 3033; light tawny 3770; light terracotta 3778; light mocha brown 3782; dark rust 3826; light rust 3827; dark mahogany 400; dark silver grey 414; med golden brown 433; light golden brown 434; light lemon 445; avocado green 469; light avocado green 470; light avocado green 471; light avocado green 472; bright orange red 606; tangerine 740; med tangerine 741; light tangerine 742; med yellow 743; light yellow 744; light yellow 745; off white 746; light terracotta 758; light yellow green 772; med cornflower blue 793; light cornflower blue 794; dark coffee brown 801; dark royal blue 820; dark coffee brown 898; dark burnt orange 900; med avocado green 937; dark coffee brown 938; tawny 945; med burnt orange 946; burnt orange 947; light tawny 951; dark rust 975; med rust 976; light rust 977

1 Read through the Techniques section if necessary, then neaten the raw edges of the fabric by pressing up a 1.5cm (⅝in) turning and stitching the hem in place. You could hand embroider to make a decorative hem on your tablecloth if you wish.

2 Follow the chart on pages 54 and 55 and work over two threads of the evenweave fabric, using two strands of stranded cotton (floss) for the cross stitch and one strand for the backstitch. Refer to the Stitch Guide on page 10 for how to work the stitches. Work the large floral garland at one corner, then stitch the various butterflies randomly above the garland and at each corner of the tablecloth (see photograph on page 51).

3 Stitch the backstitch detail using one strand of thread in black 310 to work the cat's eyes and to outline each butterfly body and wings. Use dark coffee brown 801 for the cat's mouth and light avocado green 472 for the flower stems. Work the French knots using one strand of black 310 for the ladybird spots and white for the ladybird eye.

CATNIP AND CATS

Most cats adore catnip and go mad whenever they sniff, lick or eat it. Catnip or catmint (Nepeta cataria) is a perennial plant which can be easily grown in your garden or bought from pet shops in a dried form. The smell of it drives cats wild and makes them extremely playful as well as having a relaxing effect on them too. Cats are extremely sensitive to smell and the oil found in the leaves and stems of the catnip stimulates the pathways to the brain and produces an altered state in the cat. They also like other herbs such as chives and parsley which provide them with essential minerals to keep them healthy. If they don't have fresh greenery to nibble they will eat your potted houseplants instead. Domestic cats are not the only felines attracted to catnip – lions and jaguars are also affected by it, but not tigers.

FLOWER AND BUTTERFLY NAPKINS

FINISHED DESIGN SIZES

Small floral motif
5cm (2in) square approximately

Common blue butterfly
3 x 2.5cm (1⅛ x 1in)

Large white butterfly
3.5cm (1½in) square

Small tortoiseshell butterfly
5 x 5.5cm (2 x 2¼in)

WHAT YOU WILL NEED (for each napkin)
- Cream 28-count Brittney (E3270) or other linen or evenweave fabric, 33cm (13in) square
- Matching sewing thread

DMC STRANDED COTTON (FLOSS)
Small Floral Motif

I skein: black 310; white; avocado green 469; light avocado green 470; light avocado green 471; light avocado green 472; bright orange red 606; tangerine 740; med tangerine 741; light tangerine 742; med yellow 743; light yellow 744; light yellow 745; light yellow green 772; dark burnt orange 900; med avocado green 937; med burnt orange 946; burnt orange 947

Common Blue Butterfly

I skein:: black 310; med cornflower blue 793; light cornflower blue 794

Large White Butterfly

I skein: black 310; white; dark silver grey 414; light lemon 445; off white 746

Small Tortoiseshell Butterfly

I skein: black 310; white; med golden brown 433; light golden brown 434; bright orange red 606; med tangerine 741; light tangerine 742; light yellow 745; dark royal blue 820; dark coffee brown 898

1 Read through the Techniques section if necessary, then neaten the raw edges of the fabric by pressing up a 1cm (½in) turning and stitching the hem in place. You could hand embroider to make a decorative hem on your napkins if you wish.

2 Follow the chart on pages 54 and 55, working over two threads of evenweave fabric and using two strands of stranded cotton (floss) for the cross stitch and one strand for the backstitch. Refer to the Stitch Guide on page 12 for working the stitches. Work either the small floral motif or a single butterfly at the bottom right corner of each napkin (see photograph page 51).

3 Work the backstitch detail using one strand of black 310 to outline each butterfly body and wings. Use light avocado green 472 for the flower stems. Finally, work the French knots using one strand of black 310 for the ladybird spots and white for the ladybird eye.

CATS AS COMPANIONS

The companionship of cats has been proved to be beneficial to humans. Cuddling, stroking or talking to a cat helps us to release frustration and tension, and by providing food, a warm bed and affection, a cat will give love to its owner in return. Cats soon begin to recognise and interpret the regular behaviour patterns of their owners and learn to recognise that certain sounds and actions mean they will receive food or affection. For example, when you sit down to relax with a cup of tea or after a meal, your cat will often jump onto your lap for a fuss and a snooze. They know our routine from waking to sleeping and will be waiting for us when we return home because they know they will be rewarded with affection.

FLORAL TRAY

FINISHED DESIGN SIZE
16.5 x 16.5 x 25.5cm (6½ x 6½ x 10in) approximately

WHAT YOU WILL NEED
- Cream 14-count Aida, 38cm (15in) square
- Lightweight iron-on interfacing, 38cm (15in) square
- Decorative oval tray for embroidery (available from Framecraft – see Stockists page 127)

DMC STRANDED COTTON (FLOSS)
Use the thread list for the Cat-nap Tablecloth on page 50

1 Prepare your fabric, reading through the Techniques section if necessary and marking the centre point. Following the chart on pages 54 and 55, work the large floral garland at the centre of the fabric, then work some butterflies above the garland (see photograph on page 51). The tray isn't quite large enough to accommodate the whole design so omit working the last 3cm (1¼in) at each end.

2 Use two strands of stranded cotton (floss) for the cross stitch and one strand for the backstitch. Refer to the Stitch Guide on page 12 for how to work the stitches.

3 Work the backstitch detail using one strand of black 310 to work the cat's eyes and to outline each butterfly body and wings. Use dark coffee brown 801 for the cat's mouth and light avocado green 472 for the flower stems.

4 Back your completed embroidery with iron-on interfacing, following the manufacturer's instructions. This will strengthen the fabric, prevent it from wrinkling and also help to keep the stitches secure. To complete your tray, assemble following the manufacturer's instructions.

DMC stranded cotton (floss)

	3032
	3782
	3033
	3778
	758
	938
	975
	3826
	976
	977
	3827
	945
	951
	3770
	793
	794
	414
	445
	746
	898
	433
	434
	820
	606
	937
	469
	470
	471
	472
	772
	801
	400
	900
	946
	947
	740
	741
	742
	743
	744
	745
	white
	310

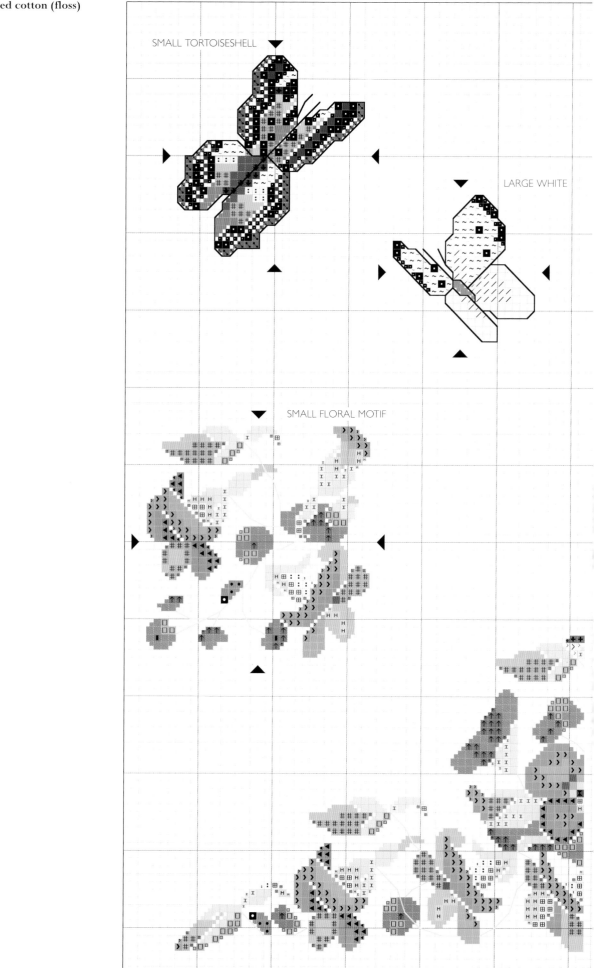

SMALL TORTOISESHELL

LARGE WHITE

SMALL FLORAL MOTIF

COMMON BLUE

LARGE FLORAL GARLAND

Emma Picture

Emma is a very pretty long-haired tortoiseshell cat and this stunning portrait of her is worked in a mixture of cross stitch, three-quarter cross stitch and backstitch, with the addition of long straight stitches to emphasise the long hairs and to soften the edges of the design. The decorative long stitches are worked over the top of the cross stitches to add detail and definition. The picture is worked on khaki 14-count Aida, but the same design could be stitched over two threads of a 28-count evenweave linen to make a stunning cushion.

FINISHED DESIGN SIZE

23cm (9in) square approximately

WHAT YOU WILL NEED

• Khaki 14-count Aida, 38cm (15in) square

DMC STRANDED COTTON (FLOSS)

1 skein: white; dark yellow beige 3045; med yellow beige 3046; light yellow beige 3047; silver grey 317; black brown 3371; light tawny 3770; dark desert sand 3772; dark pewter grey 3799; dark rust 3826; light rust 3827; dark silver grey 413; dark silver grey 414; light beige brown 543; dark desert sand 632; olive green 732; dark beige brown 838; dark beige brown 839; med beige brown 840; light beige brown 841; light beige brown 842; tawny 945; light tawny 951; dark rust 975; med rust 976; light rust 977

2 skeins: black 310

THE CAT'S WHISKERS

A cat's whiskers perform the very important function of gathering information about the surrounding environment. Whiskers are slightly wider than a cat's body, so if the whiskers can pass through a space, so can the rest of the cat. As well as the long, stiff whiskers on their cheeks, cats also have long hairs on their face, eyebrows, nose, chin and the elbows on their front legs. These are specialised hairs which have nerve endings at their roots, making each hair highly sensitive to the slightest touch or pressure. This enables cats to judge distances and spaces accurately, which is vital when they are out hunting. If its whiskers are damaged, a cat may become less confident as it is not able to sense accurately, but the whiskers soon grow back.

1 Prepare your fabric for work, reading the Techniques section if necessary and marking the centre point. Refer to the Stitch Guide on page 12 for how to work the stitches.

2 To work Emma's picture use two strands of stranded cotton (floss) for all the cross stitch. Work the backstitch using one strand of stranded cotton (floss) in black 310 around the eyes. Work the long stitches on top of the completed cross stitch, using one strand of black 310, light golden brown 977 and white for the whiskers, long hairs, eyebrows and ear hairs. Please note that the white whiskers and long hairs are shown in pale grey on the chart so they may be seen more clearly.

3 Refer to Mounting and Framing on page 11, for how to complete your picture.

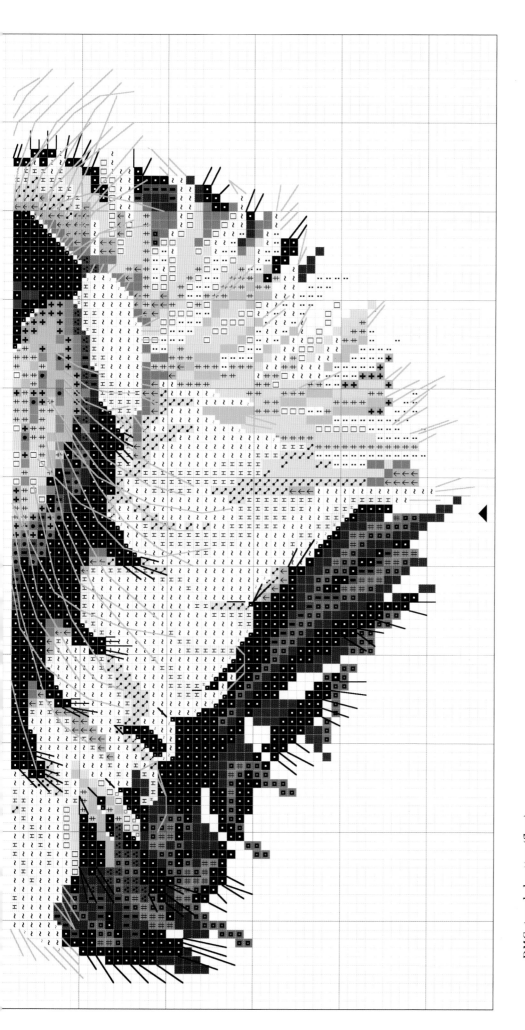

DMC stranded cotton (floss)

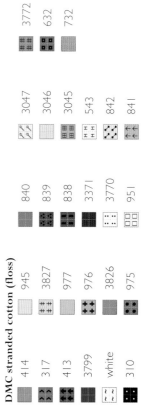

	414		945		3047		3772
	317		3827		3046		632
	413		977		3045		732
	3799		976		543		
	white		3826		842		
	310		975		841		
	840						
	839						
	838						
	3371						
	3770						
	951						

Leopard Portrait

This stunning design is a portrait of an elusive, solitary leopard resting amongst grassland foliage. The design makes an ideal companion to the tiger portrait on page 66 and, like the tiger, it is also worked in whole cross stitch with no backstitch detail, making it an ideal project to experiment with using different threads and fabrics. It could be worked in cross stitch using stranded cotton (floss) on Aida, as we have done, or in tapestry wool (yarn) on canvas – the colour key gives the shade codes for both.

FINISHED DESIGN SIZE
28 x 30cm (11 x 11¾in) approximately

WHAT YOU WILL NEED
• Summer Khaki 14-count Aida, 46cm (18in) square

DMC STRANDED COTTON (FLOSS)
1 skein: white; black 310; med mocha brown 3032; light mocha brown 3033; black brown 3371; med terracotta 356; light terracotta 3778; light terracotta 3779; light mocha brown 3782; dark rust 3826; hazelnut brown 3828; terracotta 3830; dark hazelnut brown 420; light hazelnut brown 422; med golden brown 433; light golden brown 434; light golden brown 435; tan 436; light tan 437; avocado green 469; light avocado green 470; light avocado green 471; light avocado green 472; dark drab brown 610; drab brown 611; light drab brown 612; light golden sand 676; light golden sand 677; med golden sand 729; light tan 738; light tan 739; dark coffee brown 801; light beige grey 822; dark beige brown 838; dark beige brown 839; dark hazelnut brown 869; dark coffee brown 898; black avocado green 934; dark avocado green 935; med avocado green 937; dark coffee brown 938; med rust 976; light rust 977

1 Prepare your fabric, reading through the Techniques section if necessary and marking the centre point. Refer to the Stitch Guide for how to work the stitches.

2 Follow the charts on pages 62–65, using two strands of stranded cotton (floss) for the cross stitch. If you are working the design in wool, work it in half cross stitches using one strand of tapestry wool (yarn).

3 Refer to Mounting and Framing on page 11 for how to complete your picture. (See also the photograph on page 6.)

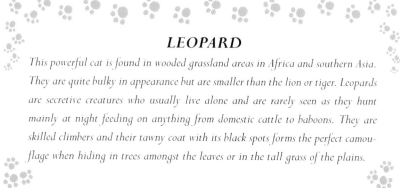

LEOPARD

This powerful cat is found in wooded grassland areas in Africa and southern Asia. They are quite bulky in appearance but are smaller than the lion or tiger. Leopards are secretive creatures who usually live alone and are rarely seen as they hunt mainly at night feeding on anything from domestic cattle to baboons. They are skilled climbers and their tawny coat with its black spots forms the perfect camou- flage when hiding in trees amongst the leaves or in the tall grass of the plains.

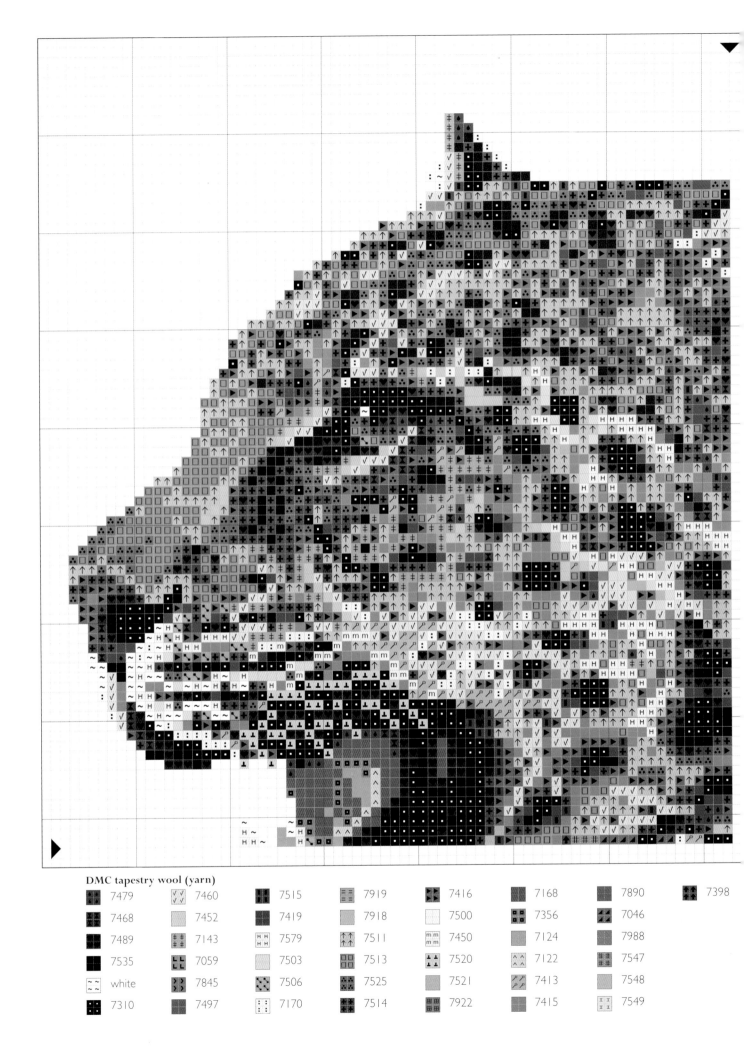

DMC tapestry wool (yarn)

7479	7460	7515	7919	7416	7168	7890	7398
7468	7452	7419	7918	7500	7356	7046	
7489	7143	7579	7511	7450	7124	7988	
7535	7059	7503	7513	7520	7122	7547	
white	7845	7506	7525	7521	7413	7548	
7310	7497	7170	7514	7922	7415	7549	

DMC stranded cotton (floss)

801	√√ 738	839	== 976	►► 610	3830	935	934
898	437	838	977	822	356	937	
938	‡‡ 436	HH 677	↑↑ 422	mm 3033	3778	469	
3371	LL 435	676	□□ 3828	↑↑ 3782	^^ 3779	## 470	
white	►► 434	729	420	3032	⁄⁄ 612	471	
310	433	∴∴ 739	869	⊞⊞ 3826	611	II 472	

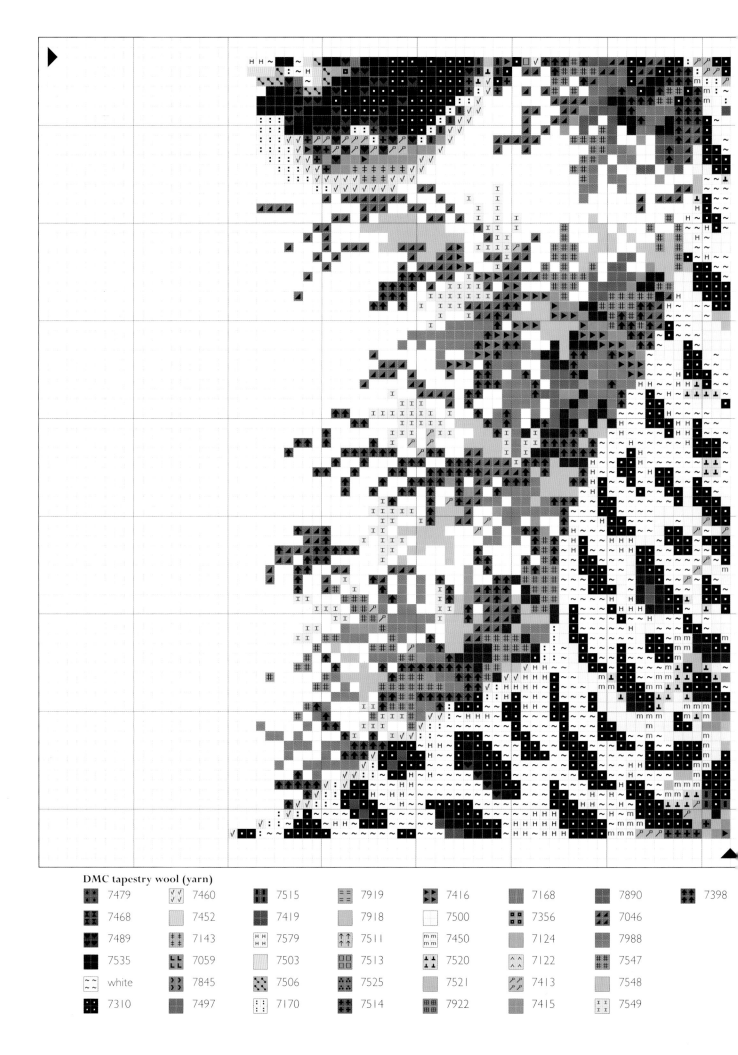

DMC tapestry wool (yarn)

7479	7460	7515	7919	7416	7168	7890	7398
7468	7452	7419	7918	7500	7356	7046	
7489	7143	7579	7511	7450	7124	7988	
7535	7059	7503	7513	7520	7122	7547	
white	7845	7506	7525	7521	7413	7548	
7310	7497	7170	7514	7922	7415	7549	

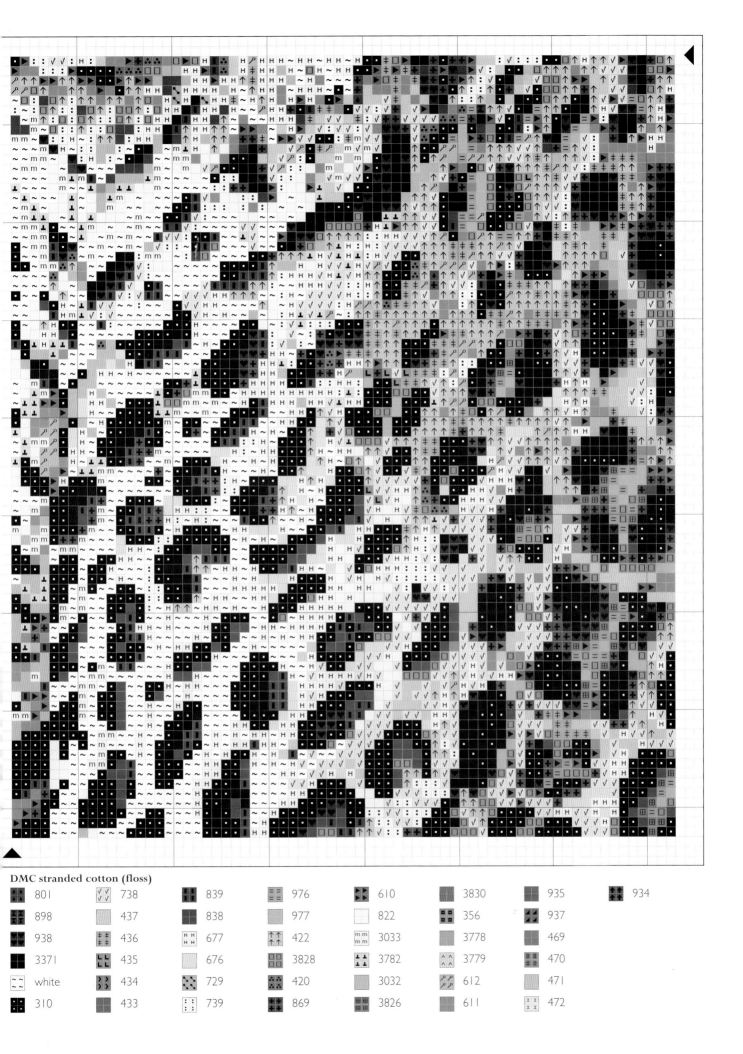

DMC stranded cotton (floss)

801	738	839	976	610	3830	935	934	
898	437	838	977	822	356	937		
938	436	677	422	3033	3778	469		
3371	435	676	3828	3782	3779	470		
white	434	729	420	3032	612	471		
310	433	739	869	3826	611	472		

Tiger Portrait

*T*igers are the biggest and most powerful of all the big cats and this design captures the
tiger in all his magnificence. The design is worked in whole cross stitch with no backstitch
detail, making it another project to experiment with using different fabrics and threads. It
could be worked in cross stitch using stranded cotton (floss) on Aida, as we have done, or in
tapestry wool (yarn) on canvas – the colour key gives the shade codes for both. This design
could be worked as a companion for the leopard portrait on page 60.

FINISHED DESIGN SIZE
37 x 33cm (14½ x 13in) approximately

WHAT YOU WILL NEED
• Summer Khaki 14-count Aida, 50cm (20in) square

DMC STRANDED COTTON (FLOSS)
1 skein: white; dark mahogany 300; black brown 3371;
light peach 352; light peach 353; dark rust 3826; light rust
3827; light avocado green 471; light avocado green 472;
light beige brown 543; light golden sand 676; light golden
sand 677; light olive green 734; off white 746; dark topaz
780; dark topaz 781; dark topaz 782; light golden olive 834;
med beige brown 840; light beige brown 841; light beige
brown 842; dark avocado green 936; med avocado green
937; dark coffee brown 938; dark rust 975; med rust 976;
light rust 977
2 skeins: black 310; black avocado green 934; dark
avocado green 935

1 Prepare your fabric, reading through the
Techniques section if necessary and marking the
centre point. Refer to the Stitch Guide for how to work
the stitches.

2 Follow the charts on pages 68–71, using two
strands of stranded cotton (floss) for the cross
stitch. If you are working the design in wool, work it
in half cross stitches using one strand of tapestry wool
(yarn).

3 Refer to Mounting and Framing on page 11 for
how to complete your picture. (See also the photograph on page 6.)

TIGER

Tigers used to be found in many of the forests of India, south-east Asia, China and as far north as Siberia, but today they are an endangered species as their natural habitat is being gradually destroyed. Their survival is being helped by special projects such as Project Tiger set up by the Indian Government. Tigers hunt alone and defend their territories from all intruders. They used to be hunted and killed because they had a reputation as man-eaters.

DMC tapestry
wool (yarn)

7470 7353 7549 7548 7046 7427 7890 7011 7762 7398 7780 7505 7783 7518 7521 7520 7450 7746 7579 7503 7917 7918 7919 7922 7401 7459 7489 7535 white 7310

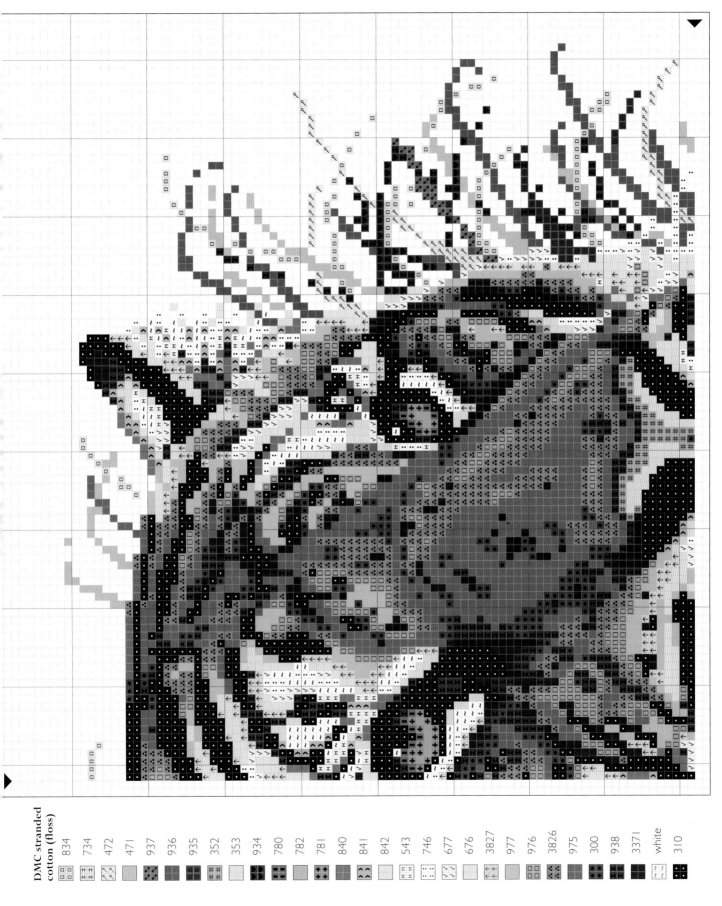

DMC stranded cotton (floss)

834 · 734 · 472 · 471 · 937 · 936 · 935 · 352 · 353 · 934 · 780 · 782 · 781 · 840 · 841 · 842 · 543 · 746 · 677 · 676 · 3827 · 977 · 976 · 3826 · 975 · 300 · 938 · 3371 · white · 310

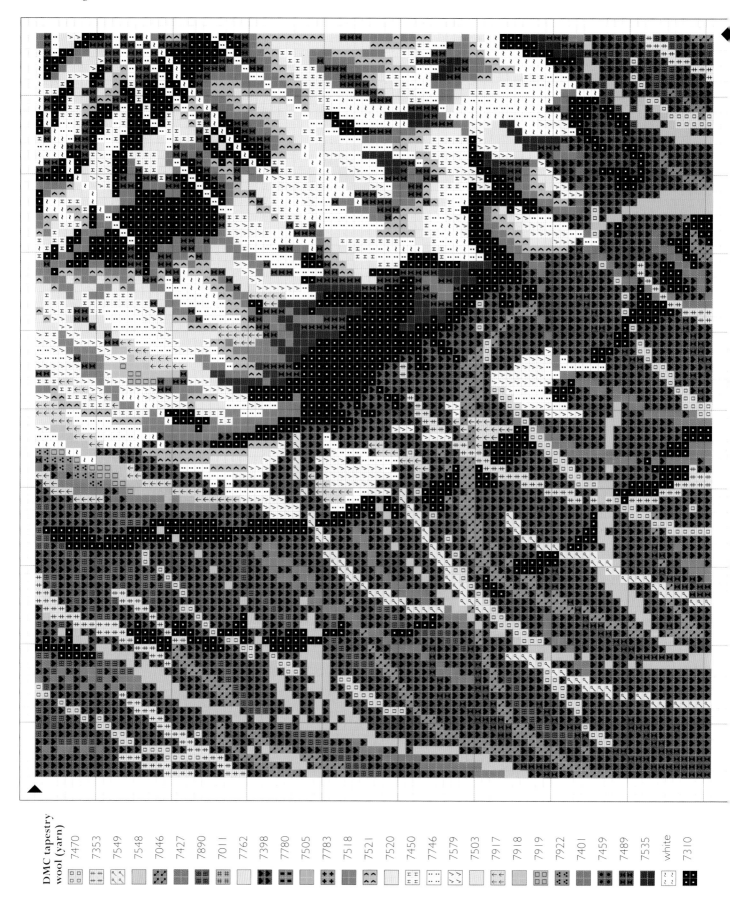

DMC stranded cotton (floss) 834 734 472 471 937 936 935 352 353 934 780 782 781 840 841 842 543 746 677 676 3827 977 976 3826 975 300 938 3371 white 310

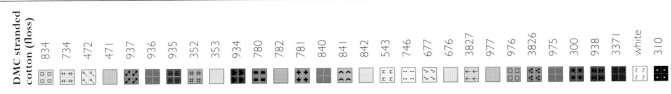

Four Seasonal Pictures

These four beautiful designs represent the four seasons. Each cat is shown with a flower common to the season with the colours of the flowers echoed in the colours of the cats' eyes. Spring is represented by a Rag Doll cat among bluebells; summer is an Exotic Shorthair with honeysuckle; autumn is a striking Abyssinian among berries and winter is a beautiful Russian Blue amid delicate snowdrops.

The designs, which can be worked individually or as a group to make up a set, are worked over two threads of 28-count even-weave linen in colours that blend well with the thread colours. Although the designs look superb as pictures, you could also work them on a larger count Aida to make a set of charming cushions, or on a smaller count to make pretty trinket boxes or cards.

SPRING

The Rag Doll

*T*he first of the four seasonal designs is this Rag Doll cat, with its beautiful bright blue
eyes highlighted by pretty bluebell flowers.

FINISHED DESIGN SIZE
19 x 22cm (7 x 8¾in) approximately

WHAT YOU WILL NEED
- Grey 28-count Cashel linen (E3281), 33 x 38cm (13 x 15in)

DMC STRANDED COTTON (FLOSS)
I skein: white; black 310; black brown 3371; light peach
352; light peach 353; light pistachio green 368; light blue
violet 3747; cornflower blue 3807; light straw 3822; light
golden brown 433; light golden brown 434; light golden
brown 435; tan 436; light tan 437; light beige brown 543;
cream 712; light tan 738; light tan 739; dark cornflower
blue 792; med cornflower blue 793; light cornflower blue
794; dark coffee brown 801; light blue 813; med blue
826; light blue 827; med beige brown 840; light beige
brown 841; light beige brown 842; dark coffee brown
938

1 Prepare your fabric for work, reading the
Techniques section if necessary and marking the
centre point. Refer to the Stitch Guide on page 12 for
how to work the stitches.

2 Use two strands of stranded cotton (floss) for the
cross stitch and one strand for the backstitch,
worked over two threads of the evenweave. Use one
strand for the French knots and long stitches. Work
backstitch detail in black 310 around the cat's eyes and
dark cornflower blue 792 for the flower detail. Use one
strand of light straw 3822 to work French knots for the
flower stamens and one strand of white to work long
stitches for the whiskers and eyebrows.

3 Refer to Mounting and Framing on page 11 for
how to complete your picture.

THE RAG DOLL
*These docile cats are a cross breed of Persian and
Birman and are poplar in America but rare in England
and Europe. They are large with long hair and tufted
paws and are popular partly because their temperament
makes them ideal pets for children. They were originally bred in California and were given their name
because when picked up they hang completely limp, like
a rag doll. Two other characteristics of the breed are
that they don't fight with other animals, and that they
have a very high tolerance to pain, which can be dan-
gerous because any serious injuries may go unnoticed.
Some breeders argue that the extreme docility and tolerance of pain is not in the best interests of the cat and
some have tried to breed cats which look the same but
without these characteristics.*

This charming design of a Rag Doll cat is worked using a mixture of cross stitch, three-quarter cross stitch,
backstitch and French knots, on a pale grey linen which enhances the blue shades used for the
eyes and flowers.

75

Spring - The Rag Doll   DMC stranded cotton (floss)

826	842	433	738	793	3822
813	841	801	437	794	368
827	840	938	436	3747	792
white	352	3371	435	712	3807
310	353	543	434	739	

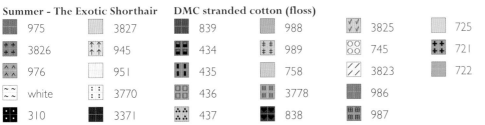

Summer - The Exotic Shorthair   ### DMC stranded cotton (floss)

	975		3827		839		988		3825		725	
	3826		945		434		989		745		721	
	976		951		435		758		3823		722	
	white		3770		436		3778		986			
	310		3371		437		838		987			

SUMMER

The Exotic Shorthair

The season of summer is depicted by this stunning portrait of an exotic shorthair cat among honeysuckle. These beautiful cats have a soft, dense coat with medium length fur which stands out and makes them look really fluffy. The large, round eyes echo the warm colours of the flowers.

FINISHED DESIGN SIZE
19 x 22cm (7 x 8¾in) approximately

WHAT YOU WILL NEED
• Sage 28-count Quaker linen (E3993), 33 x 38cm (13 x 15in)

DMC STRANDED COTTON (FLOSS)
I skein: white; black 310; black brown 3371; light tawny 3770; light terracotta 3778; light yellow 3823; light pumpkin 3825; dark rust 3826; dark rust 3827; light golden brown 434; light golden brown 435; tan 436; light tan 437; med orange spice 721; med orange spice 722; topaz 725; light yellow 745; light terracotta 758; dark beige brown 838; dark beige brown 839; tawny 945; light tawny 951; dark rust 975; med rust 976; dark forest green 986; dark forest green 987; med forest green 988; forest green 989

1 Prepare your fabric for work, reading through the Techniques section if necessary and marking the centre point. Refer to the Stitch Guide on page 12 for how to work the stitches.

2 Use two strands of stranded cotton (floss) for the cross stitch and one strand for the backstitch, worked over two threads of the evenweave linen. Use one strand for the long stitches. Work the backstitch detail using one strand of black 310 around the cat's eyes, light golden brown 435 for the flower stamens and around the flower petals and two strands of light golden brown 434 for the flower stems. Finally use one strand of white to work the long stitches for the whiskers and eyebrows.

3 Refer to Mounting and Framing on page 11 for how to complete your picture.

THE EXOTIC SHORTHAIR
These distinctive cats with their solid body, short bushy tail, round face, snub nose, and large, round golden eyes were first bred in America in the 1960s. A programme of selective breeding was developed to produce a cat that looked like a Persian but had a manageable coat that didn't need constant brushing and attention. American breeders crossed a Persian with an American shorthair to develop a sturdy cat with a dense fluffy coat, who was playful and alert with a calm and affectionate personality. Altogether there are about forty varieties of exotic shorthairs in all coat colours and patterns.

This beautiful design of an Exotic Shorthair is worked in silk threads using subtle shades of beige, golden browns and cream to create the cat's honey-coloured coat. The colouring of the large, round golden eyes are echoed in the rich orange, gold and yellow of the honeysuckle flowers. The design is worked on sage green 28-count linen which forms a perfect colour contrast.

79

AUTUMN

The Abyssinian

This autumn design shows the head of an elegant Abyssinian cat amongst seasonal berries and foliage. The rusty tones of the cinnamon-coloured fur are beautifully highlighted by the deep shades of the orange and red bryony berries. These distinctive cats have almond-shaped amber eyes, with fur in many colours.

FINISHED DESIGN SIZE
19 x 22cm (7 x 8¾in) approximately

WHAT YOU WILL NEED
• Desert Sand 28-count Cashel linen (E3281), 33 x 38cm (13 x 15in)

DMC STRANDED COTTON (FLOSS)
I skein: white; black 310; dark mocha brown 3031; med mocha brown 3032; light mocha brown 3033; dark yellow beige 3045; med yellow beige 3046; light yellow beige 3047; light terracotta 3778; dark mocha brown 3781; light mocha brown 3782; dark rust 3826; hazelnut brown 3828; dark hazelnut brown 420; light hazelnut brown 422; bright orange red 606; light golden sand 676; light golden sand 677; olive green 732; med olive green 733; light olive green 734; tangerine 740; off white 746; light terracotta 758; dark garnet 814; dark coral red 817; dark golden olive 829; dark hazelnut brown 869; med rust 976; light rust 977

1 Prepare your fabric for work, reading the Techniques section if necessary and marking the centre point. Refer to the Stitch Guide on page 12 for how to work the stitches.

2 Use two strands of stranded cotton (floss) for the cross stitch and one strand for the backstitch,
worked over two threads of evenweave linen. Work the backstitch detail in black 310 around the cat's eyes and dark mocha brown 3031 for the bryony stems. Use one strand of white to work small French knots for the berry highlights, and finally use one strand of white to work the long stitches for the whiskers and eyebrows.

3 Refer to Mounting and Framing on page 11 for how to complete your picture.

THE ABYSSINIAN
In 1868 a male cat called Zulu was bought to Britain by some soldiers returning from the war in Abyssinia, known today as Ethiopia. Zulu was used to start a breeding programme and in 1882 the breed was recognised in Britain. Although they are now available in many colours including blue, fawn and silver, their original brown and light copper colouring was similar to the colour of a wild hare or rabbit, which resulted in them being called names like Hare Cat, Rabbit Cat and Bunny Cat. Although no one knows exactly where this breed originally comes from, it is thought that they could be descendants of the sacred cats of Egypt as they look like the cats depicted on tomb paintings found in Ancient Egypt.

Cross stitch, three-quarter cross stitch, backstitch and French knots are used to work this elegant Abyssinian cat.
The subtle sand-coloured 28-count linen, forms a perfect background for the autumnal shades used.

81

Autumn - The Abyssinian   **DMC stranded cotton (floss)**

3045	977	746	3032	732	814
3046	869	3778	3782	733	817
3047	420	758	3033	734	606
white	3828	3826	676	3031	740
310	422	976	677	3781	829

Winter - The Russian Blue   DMC stranded cotton (floss)

■	317	○○	563 €	⊥⊥	3772	⊞⊞	320 F	▲▲	367 F
■	413	⁄⁄	762	■	632	■	368 F		
■	3799	⁴⁴	415		838	‡‡	369 F		
~~	white		318	■	561 €		927		
■	310	⊞⊞	414		562 €/F	∷∷	928		

WINTER

The Russian Blue

*The final design in the seasonal pictures collection shows a beautiful Russian Blue
sitting amid a bunch of delicate snowdrops. The white flower petals and the green
leaves and stems echo the cat's eyes with their green and turquoise shades
and white highlights.*

FINISHED DESIGN SIZE
19 x 22cm (7 x 8¾in) approximately

WHAT YOU WILL NEED
• Delft Blue 28-count Cashel linen (E3281),
33 x 38cm (13 x 15in)

DMC STRANDED COTTON (FLOSS)
I skein: white; black 310; silver grey 317; light silver grey
318; med pistachio green 320; dark pistachio green 367;
light pistachio green 368; light pistachio green 369; dark
desert sand 3772; dark pewter grey 3799; dark silver grey
413; dark silver grey 414; silver grey 415; dark jade 561;
med jade 562; light jade 563; dark desert sand 632; light
pearl grey 762; dark beige brown 838; light grey green 927;
light grey green 928

1 Prepare your fabric for work, reading the
Techniques section if necessary and marking the
centre point. Refer to the Stitch Guide on page 12 for
how to work the stitches.

2 Use two strands of stranded cotton (floss) for the
cross stitch and one strand for the backstitch,
worked over two threads of evenweave linen. Use
one strand of stranded cotton (floss) for the long
stitches. Work backstitch detail in black 310 around

the cat's eyes and light pistachio green 369 for the
upper flower stems. Work backstitch detail using two
strands of med pistachio green 320 for the lower
plant stems, and finally use one strand of black 310 to
work the long stitches for the whiskers and eyebrows.

3 Refer to Mounting and Framing on page 11 for
how to complete your picture.

THE RUSSIAN BLUE
*The Russian Blue is one of the most aristocratic cats of
the cat world. They became popular in the nineteenth
century when it was fashionable to own and exhibit
exotic cats. Queen Victoria became a patron of these
exhibitions and owned two Russian Blues herself, whilst
Tsar Nicholas I owned a very famous one called Vashka.
These cats are thought to have been introduced to
Europe in the 1860s by British sailors returning from
Archangel, a port in northern Russia. They are known
by many names such as Archangel Blues, Maltese Blues,
Spanish Blues, Chartreuse Blues and British Blues.
These beautiful cats prefer to live in quiet surroundings
with little disturbance or noise. They are affectionate
and loving towards each other and make good parents.*

The rich, deep blue-grey coat of this Russian Blue, with its plush, dense fur is worked in silk threads using shades
of pewter, silver grey, steel grey and black. The design is worked using cross stitch, three-quarter cross stitch
and backstitch on 28-count linen in a subtle shade of Delft blue, which forms a perfect background
for both the cat and snowdrops.

85

Lion Cubs Picture

Lion cubs are irresistible and we think you'll find this design irresistible too. It has been worked into a picture of two adorable cub faces peeping out from foliage. Cross stitch and three-quarter cross stitch are used to work the design with the addition of long stitches for whiskers and eyebrows. It has been worked on a subtle shade of light grey Aida which blends with the design but you could use a darker colour to give it a completely different look. Alternatively you could work one of the faces on a smaller count Aida or linen to decorate a trinket box, or on a larger count to make a cushion.

FINISHED DESIGN SIZE

20 x 34cm (7³/₄ x 13¹/₂in) approximately

WHAT YOU WILL NEED

• Barn Grey14-count Aida, 35 x 48cm (14 x 19in)

DMC STRANDED COTTON (FLOSS)

I skein: white; black 310; dark pine green 3362; med pine green 3363; pine green 3364; black brown 3371; med golden brown 433; light golden brown 434; light golden brown 435; tan 436; light tan 437; cream 712; light tan 738; light tan 739; dark topaz 780; dark coffee brown 801; dark coffee brown 898; dark coffee brown 938

1 Prepare your fabric for work, reading the Techniques section if necessary and marking the centre point. Refer to the Stitch Guide on page 12 for how to work the stitches.

2 Use two strands of stranded cotton (floss) for the cross stitch and two strands for the long stitches. When the cross stitching is complete, use white to work long stitches for the lion cubs' whiskers and eyebrows.

3 Refer to Mounting and Framing on page 11 for how to complete your picture.

LION CUBS

Females lions outnumber the males in a pride and each lioness gives birth to four or five cubs every two years. When the cubs reach maturity the females often stay with the family group but the young males either gain a place in the pride by ousting an older lion or join another pride which is in need of males.

DMC stranded cotton (floss)

■ 3371	▨ 801	▨ 435	▨ 738	▨ 780	▨ 3364
～ white	■ 898	▶ 434	↑↑ 437	⋮⋮ 712	▨ 3363
▨ 310	■ 938	▨ 433	436	H H 739	▶▶ 3362

Chinchilla Bell Pull

The distinctive appearance of these popular long-haired cats has been captured in this stunning design worked on 14-count black Aida which helps to accentuate the long, white, shimmering coat and the stunning green eyes. A mixture of cross stitch, three-quarter cross stitch, backstitch and long stitches are used to work the design which has been made into a bell pull. Alternatively, the design would look wonderful worked as a tall picture on linen fabric.

FINISHED DESIGN SIZE

15 x 40cm (5¾ x 16in) approximately

WHAT YOU WILL NEED

- Black 14-count Aida, 30 x 60cm (12 x 24in)
- Cotton backing fabric, 30 x 90cm (³/₈yd x 36in) wide
- Contrast furnishing braid, 1.5m (1⁵/₈yd)
- Matching sewing thread
- Bell pull hanging rod, 20cm (8in) long (available from Framecraft – see Stockists page 127)

DMC STRANDED COTTON (FLOSS)

1 skein: black 310; silver grey 317; light peach 352; light peach 353; light tawny 3770; med desert sand 3773; dark shell grey 451; med shell grey 452; light shell grey 453; light emerald green 912; light emerald green 913; light desert sand 950; peppermint green 954; light peppermint green 955; dark forest green 986; med forest green 988; forest green 989

2 skeins: white; light pearl grey 762

1 Prepare your fabric, reading through the Techniques section if necessary and marking the centre point. The length of the bell pull hanging rod determines the width of the fabric. Our hanging rod allows for a 19cm (7½in) wide strip and 6mm (¼in) wide braid. Purchase the rod before you start working the design to ensure that it will be wide enough.

2 Refer to the Stitch Guide on page 12 for how to work the stitches. Use two strands of stranded cotton (floss) for the cross stitch and one strand for the backstitch and the long stitches. Work backstitch detail in black 310 around the eyes and nose and work long stitches in white for the whiskers. When you have completed the stitching, press.

TO MAKE THE BELL PULL

1 Mark the correct width and length of the bell pull on to the embroidered fabric with tacking (basting) lines. Cut the fabric, adding 1.5cm (⁵/₈in) along both long and diagonal edges and 5cm (2in) at the top edge. Press turnings in place, mitring the corners (see fig 8). Cut the backing fabric to the same size but add a 1.5cm (⁵/8in) turning all the way round.

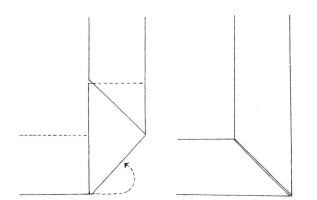

Fig 8   Mitring corners

2 Using matching sewing thread, hand stitch the turnings in place along both long and diagonal edges of the embroidered fabric, then hand stitch furnishing braid around the turned edges.

3 Position the hanging rod at the top of the strip, on the wrong side under the fold of the turnings, then stitch the backing fabric into place to finish.

THE CHINCHILLA

The Chinchilla is a variation of the Persian and is distinguished by the white, sparkly coat, bright green eyes and brick red nose. The hairs on the head, back, legs and tail are tipped with black which makes their white coats seem to shimmer. The hairs on the underparts are pure white. The pretty face is exaggerated by the black outlines around the eyes and nose, as though the cat is wearing eyeliner and mascara. Most people are familiar with the Chinchilla breed because they appear in the James Bond films at the side of the arch enemy of 007.

DMC stranded
cotton (floss)

▲▲	986
	988
❭❭	989
	3773
‖‖	950
	352
√√	353
⦿⦿	317
	451
▫▫	452
⋮⋮	453
H H	762
	3770
	912
# #	913
	954
⋮⋮	955
~ ~	white
⦙⦙	310

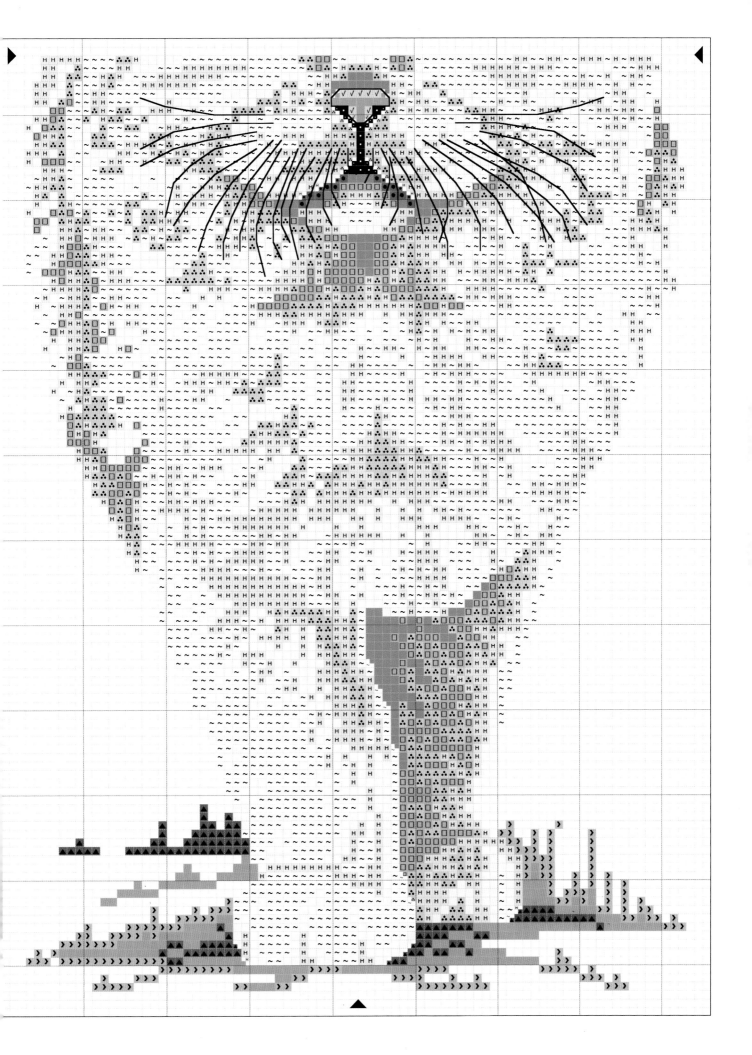

Cats in a Row

This irresistible collection of kittens features a mixture of breeds from pedigree to moggie and shows how unique cats are. These colourful kittens all in a row make a charming and versatile design, stitched in a mixture of cross stitch, three-quarter cross stitch and back-stitch. We have worked the design on 16-count Aida, working each stitch over two blocks and making it up as a draught excluder. We have also worked part of the design as a picture, only stitching the two fluffy Persian kittens, but the whole design would also look charming made up as a long picture.

CATS IN A ROW PICTURE

FINISHED DESIGN SIZE
15 x 20.5cm (6 x 8in) approximately

WHAT YOU WILL NEED
• Black 14-count Aida, 30 x 36cm (12 x 14in)

DMC STRANDED COTTON (FLOSS)
I skein: black 310; white; dark khaki green 3011; med khaki green 3012; light khaki green 3013; light mocha brown 3033; black brown 3371; light peach 352; light peach 353; light tawny 3770; dark rust 3826; light rust 3827; hazelnut brown 3828; tan 436; light tan 437; light golden sand 677; light tan 738; light tan 739; off white 746; dark coffee brown 801; med beige brown 840; light beige brown 841; light beige brown 842; dark hazelnut brown 869; dark coffee brown 938; tawny 945; light tawny 951; dark rust 975; med rust 976; light rust 977

FRIEND OR FOE

Although strongly independent, cats are also very sociable creatures and need company and stimulation. Just as we need cats for companionship, they need our company too. We don't realise what an enormous shock it is for a tiny kitten to be taken from its mother and put in a strange environment on its own, where it no longer has the company of its littermates, no one to play with and no mother to cuddle up to. The kitten relies on us to provide it with love, companionship and stimulation. Another kitten is ideal company and cats introduced to each other when they are kittens are usually friends for life. If a cat is left alone all day it will become bored and unhappy and will play with anything it can find, usually furniture, carpets or wallpaper! If you want your kitten to grow into a happy and contented cat, provide it with lots of love and stimulation.

1 Prepare the black Aida fabric for work, reading the Techniques section if necessary and marking the centre point of the fabric. Refer to the Stitch Guide on page 12 for how to work the stitches. Follow the chart given on page 99, but use only part of the design – that with the ginger and cream fluffy Persian kittens near the right end of the design (check with the photograph above).

2 When stitching the design use two strands of stranded cotton (floss) for the cross stitch and one strand for the backstitch and French knots. Work backstitch detail in black 310 around each cat's eyes, and work a French knot in white for each eye highlight.

3 Refer to Mounting and Framing on page 11 for how to complete your picture.

CATS IN A ROW DRAUGHT EXCLUDER

FINISHED DESIGN SIZE

28 x 79cm (11 x 31in) approximately

WHAT YOU WILL NEED

- Light Sand 16-count Aida (E3251), 43 x 94cm (17 x 37in)
- Heavyweight cotton backing fabric, 40cm x 115cm (¹/₂yd x 45in) wide
- Medium-weight iron-on interfacing, 40cm x 115cm (¹/₂yd x 45in) wide
- Polyester wadding (batting) for filling
- Matching sewing thread

1 Prepare your fabric for work, reading the Techniques section if necessary and marking the centre point. Refer to the Stitch Guide on page 12 for how to work the stitches.

DMC STRANDED COTTON (FLOSS)

I skein: dark khaki green 3011; med khaki green 3012; light khaki green 3013; med mocha brown 3032; light mocha brown 3033; light beaver grey 3072; silver grey 317; light silver grey 318; black brown 3371; light peach 352; light peach 353; med Wedgwood blue 3760; light tawny 3770; dark mocha brown 3781; light mocha brown 3782; dark pewter grey 3799; dark rust 3826; light rust 3827; hazelnut brown 3828; dark silver grey 413; dark silver grey 414; silver grey 415; dark hazelnut brown 420; light hazelnut brown 422; tan 436; light tan 437; dark Wedgwood blue 517; light beige brown 543; dark beaver grey 646; med beaver grey 647; light beaver grey 648; light golden sand 677; light tan 738; light pearl grey 762; dark coffee brown 801; med beige brown 840; light beige brown 841; light beige brown 842; dark hazelnut brown 869; dark coffee brown 938; tawny 945; light tawny 951; dark rust 975; med rust 976; light rust 977

2 skeins: black 310; white; light tan 739; off white 746

2 Follow the chart on pages 98–99 and stitch the design using three strands of stranded cotton (floss) for the cross stitch and two strands for the backstitch and French knots, working over two blocks of Aida. Work backstitch detail in black 310 around each cat's eyes, and then work a French knot in white for each eye highlight.

3 When the design is complete, back the embroidered fabric with medium-weight iron-on interfacing (follow the manufacturer's instructions) to strengthen the fabric and help keep the stitches secure. Using a soft pencil, draw a line all around the design, measuring 5cm (2in) from the finished embroidery. Cut away excess fabric along the line.

4 Cut a piece of backing fabric to the same size and shape as the embroidered fabric. With right sides facing, place the front and back pieces together, then pin and tack (baste) around the edges. Machine stitch

the layers together, taking a 1.5cm (⅝in) seam allowance and leaving a 30cm (12in) gap along the bottom edge for turning.

5 Trim away any excess fabric and clip into the seams where necessary then turn through to the right side. Fill the draught excluder with polyester wadding (batting), then secure the gap with slipstitching.

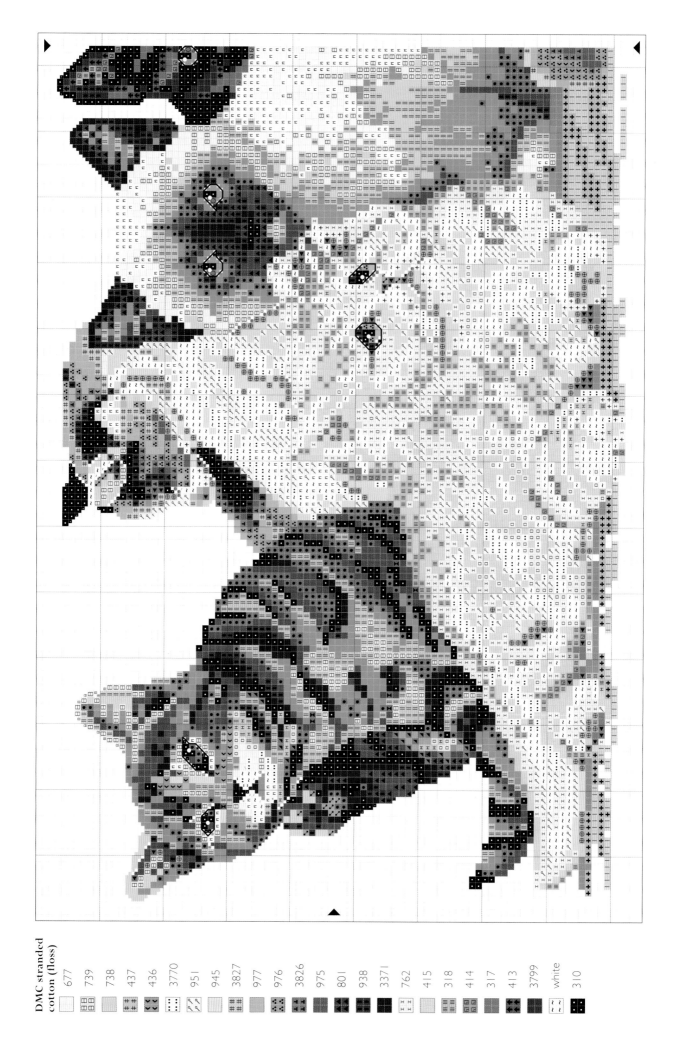

DMC stranded
cotton (floss)

677
739
738
437
436
3770
951
945
3827
977
976
3826
975
801
938
3371
762
415
318
414
317
413
3799
white
310

	3013	3012	3011	3033	3782	3032	3781	3760	517	543	842	841	840	353	352	3072	648	647	646	422	3828	420	869	746

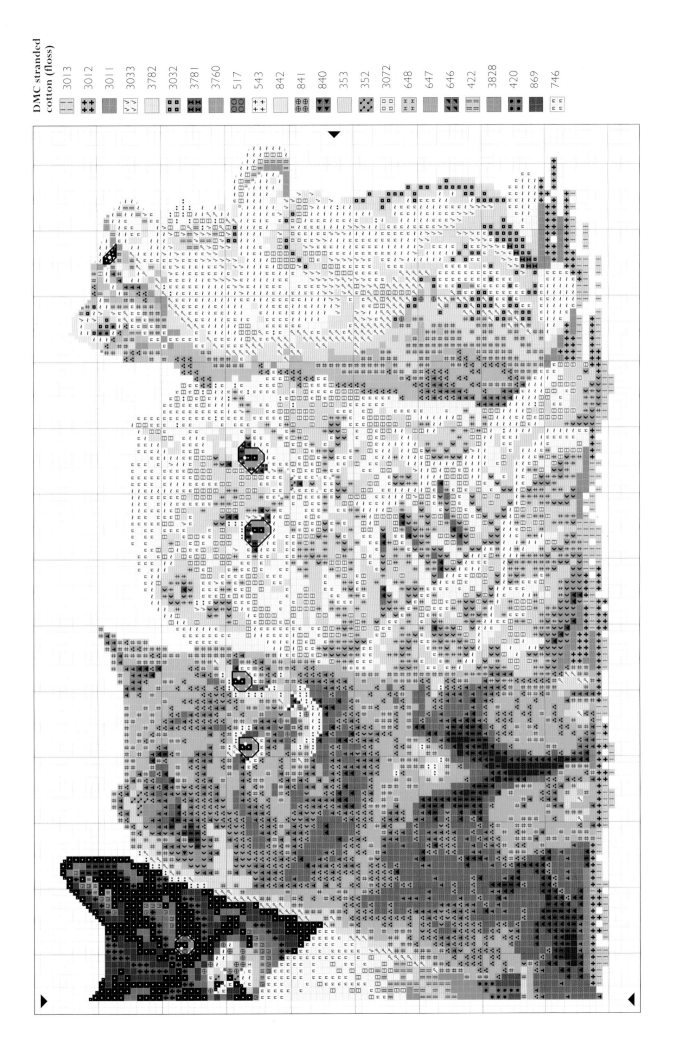

Panther Portrait

The black panther is a striking creature which is rarely seen and so we decided to include this stunning portrait in our collection of cats from around the world. The design is worked in whole cross stitch throughout, in a mixture of subtle tones of black and grey, with small splashes of colour for the mouth and the amber eyes. This beautiful design is worked on black Aida so the elusive panther gently merges with the background. Because it is worked in whole cross stitch, it is ideal for experimenting with different fabrics such as different counts of Aida or evenweave linen.

PANTHER

Many people believe that the black panther is a separate species of big cat, however, if you look closely at the coat of a panther you can see a subtle pattern of spots, because a panther is in fact just a leopard with hidden spots. The black colouring of the panther's coat is a gene variation which can occur in many other species from the jaguar to the domestic moggie. Panthers behave just like spotted leopards and breed freely with them. This colour variation of the leopard coat is most common in the forests of south-east Asia.

FINISHED DESIGN SIZE
24 x 33cm (9½ x 13in) approximately

WHAT YOU WILL NEED
• Black 14-count Aida, 38 x 48cm (15 x 19in)

DMC STRANDED COTTON (FLOSS)
1 skein: black 310; white; med yellow beige 3046; light yellow beige 3047; silver grey 317; light silver grey 318; med terracotta 356; light terracotta 3778; light terracotta 3779; dark silver grey 414; silver grey 415; light golden sand 677; off white 746; light terracotta 758; light pearl grey 762; dark coffee brown 801; med golden olive 831; golden olive 832; light golden olive 833
2 skeins: dark pewter grey 3799; dark silver grey 413
3 skeins: black 310 (optional)

1 Prepare your fabric, reading through the Techniques and Stitch Guide sections if necessary and marking the centre point.

2 Use two strands of stranded cotton (floss) for the cross stitch. If working on black Aida, to save time you could omit stitching the areas of cross stitch using black stranded cotton (floss).

3 Refer to Mounting and Framing on page 11 for how to complete your picture.

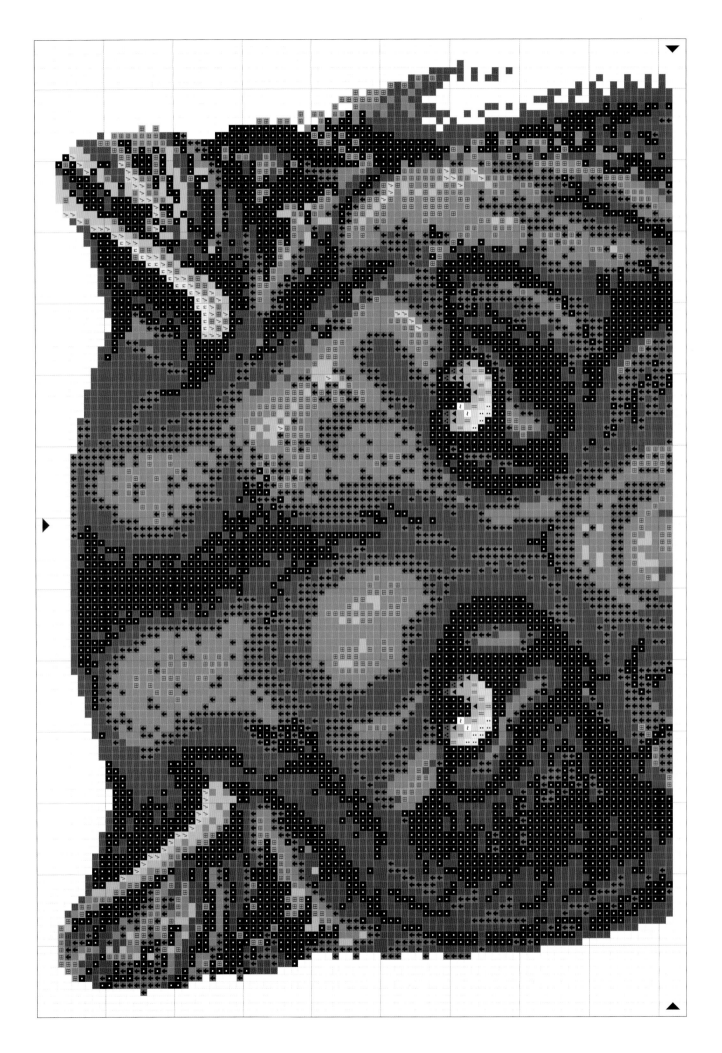

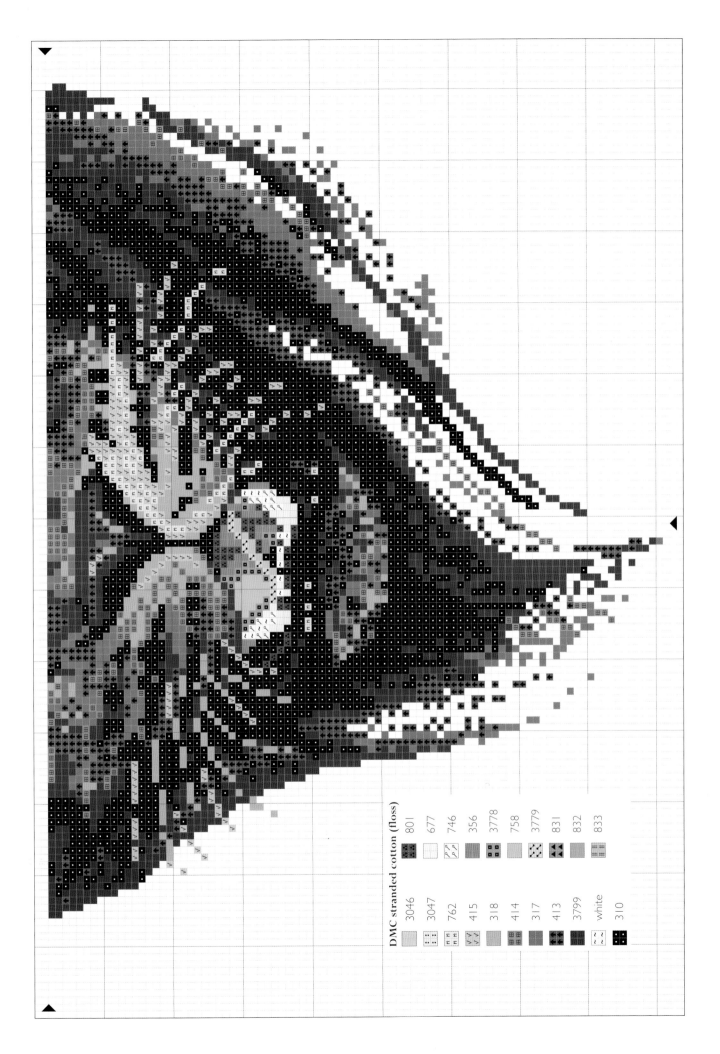

DMC stranded cotton (floss)

3046	801		
3047	677		
762	746		
415	356		
318	3778		
414	758		
317	3779		
413	831		
3799	832		
white	833		
310			

Spots and Stripes

These stunning designs are abstract representations of tiger stripes and leopard spots, worked into striking cushions and a magnificent rug. Both designs are stitched in whole cross stitch so that they can be worked in silk threads or wool. The cushions are worked in both stranded cotton (floss) on Aida and tapestry wool (yarn) on canvas. They may look like a lot of work but if you use black Aida you only need to stitch the colours and not the black areas. The rug is a labour of love and takes a lot of stitching but the results are more than worth the effort.

SILK THREAD CUSHIONS

FINISHED DESIGN SIZE
40.5cm (16in) square approximately

WHAT YOU WILL NEED
- Black 14-count Aida, 56cm (22in) square
- Light-weight iron-on interfacing 56cm (22in) square
- Cotton fabric for backing, 30 x 90cm (³/₈yd x 36in) wide
- Thick furnishing braid, 2.5m (2 ³/₄yd)
- Matching sewing thread
- Square cushion pad to fit

DMC STRANDED COTTON (FLOSS)
Leopard spots
1 skein: white; dark hazelnut brown 420; dark golden sand 680; dark hazelnut brown 869

2 skeins: dark golden sand 3829; off white 746

3 skeins: light golden sand 676; light golden sand 677

4 skeins: med golden sand 729

Tiger stripes
1 skein: white; dark mahogany 300; light rust 3827; light golden sand 676; light golden sand 677; off white 746; med rust 976; light rust 977

2 skeins: dark rust 975

4 skeins: dark rust 3826

1 Prepare your fabric for work, reading the Techniques and Stitch Guide sections if necessary and marking the centre point.

2 Use two strands of stranded cotton (floss) to work the cross stitch but do not work the black areas of the chart.

3 Following the relevant spots or stripes chart on pages 110–113, work the central panel of the cushion. When the central section is complete leave a border ten rows wide all around.

4 Work the outer border using the border section charted on page 110 or 112. Begin at the top

left-hand corner and keep repeating until you have worked all round the central panel (see fig 9).

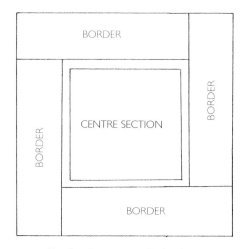

Fig 9   Positioning the borders

TO MAKE UP THE CUSHION

1 For the cushion front, follow the manufacturer's instructions to back the embroidery with light-weight iron-on interfacing. Trim away excess fabric to within 1.5cm (⁵/₈in) of the stitches leaving an embroidered square with a 1.5cm (⁵/₈in) seam allowance.

2 For the cushion back, cut two pieces of cotton fabric 26.5 x 43.5cm (10¹/₂ x 17¹/₄in), then take each rectangle and hem along one long edge. Lay the embroidered fabric face upwards on a flat surface. With right sides down, lay the two rectangles over the front so that all the raw edges match and the hemmed edges overlap at the centre. Pin, tack (baste) and machine stitch the layers together, along the stitching line. Turn the cover through to the right side.

3 Add a tasselled braid edging to the cushion. Cut the furnishing braid into four equal lengths and hand stitch a length along each cushion edge, leaving equal lengths of braid extended at each end. Pinch together the two lengths of braid extending from each corner, then use matching sewing thread to tightly bind them together. Secure the sewing thread with a knot then fray the braid to make a tassel (see fig 1 page 16).

TAPESTRY WOOL CUSHIONS

FINISHED DESIGN SIZE
56cm (22in) square approximately

WHAT YOU WILL NEED
- Double mesh 10-count canvas (E1231), 90cm (36in) square
- Medium-weight iron-on interfacing, 60 x 90cm (³/₄yd x 36in) wide
- Cotton fabric for backing, 60 x 90cm (³/₄yd x 36in) wide
- Matching sewing thread
- Polyester wadding (batting) for filling cushion

DMC TAPESTRY WOOL (YARN), 8m (8³/₄yd) SKEINS
Leopard spots

2 skeins: white; dark hazelnut brown 7845; dark hazelnut brown 7497

3 skeins: dark golden sand 7846; off white 7746

4 skeins: dark golden sand 7508

6 skeins: light golden sand 7453

7 skeins: light golden sand 7739

8 skeins: med golden sand 7455

19 skeins: black 7310

Tiger stripes

2 skeins: white; dark mahogany 7459; light rust 7917; light golden sand 7739; light golden sand 7453; off white 7746; light rust 7918

3 skeins: med rust 7919

5 skeins: dark rust 7401

9 skeins: dark rust 7922

25 skeins: black 7310

1 Prepare your canvas for work as for Aida or even-weave fabric, reading through Techniques if necessary. Canvas tends to stretch and lose its shape easily, so to prevent this and make working easier mount it on to a large frame and mark the centre point.

2 Follow the relevant spots or stripes chart on pages 110–113. Work in half cross stitch with one strand of tapestry wool (yarn). Refer to the Stitch Guide for how to work half cross stitch. Use a large tapestry needle and a thimble to protect your fingers.

3 To work the design, follow steps 3 and 4 of the silk thread cushions on page 106. You will need to work the black border for the wool cushion.

TO MAKE UP THE CUSHION

1 For the cushion front, follow the manufacturer's instructions to back the embroidery with medium-weight iron-on interfacing. Trim away excess canvas to within 1.5cm (⁵/₈in) of the stitches, leaving an embroidered square with a 1.5cm (⁵/₈in) seam allowance.

2 Cut a square of cotton backing fabric to the same size as the cushion front. With right sides facing and raw edges matching, pin, tack (baste) and machine stitch the layers together along the stitching line leaving a 30cm (12in) gap along one edge. Turn the cover through to the right side, fill with polyester wadding (batting) and secure the gap with slipstitches.

SPOTS AND STRIPES

The patterns and markings of the big cats' fur coats are stunning to look at and because of this they have been hunted for hundreds of years to make coats and luxury items. It is easy to see why these coats are so attractive to us but thankfully people are beginning to realise that it is cruel to kill animals just for their fur. The fur has many uses for the cat and is very important to its survival. It not only keeps the cat warm but also forms a camouflage in its natural environment, carries their scent and acts as a touch sensor, as the sensitive hair roots mean that each hair is highly sensitive to touch. Their coats are made up from two layers of fur — the short, soft, downy fur of the undercoat is covered by an outer layer of longer coarse hairs. It is this top coat which forms the spotted or striped pattern.

TIGER STRIPES RUG

FINISHED DESIGN SIZE

117cm (46in) square approximately

WHAT YOU WILL NEED

- Sudan 7-count interlock canvas (E699), 3m (3¼yd)
- Tapestry needle
- Thimble
- Sewing thread

DMC TAPESTRY WOOL (YARN), 8m (8³/₄yd) SKEINS

5 skeins: white

8 skeins: off white 7746

10 skeins: light golden sand 7453; dark mahogany 7459; light rust 7917

11 skeins: light golden sand 7739

12 skeins: light rust 7918

15 skeins: med rust 7919

27 skeins: dark rust 7401

50 skeins: dark rust 7922

28 hanks (38m/41¹/₂yd): black 7310

1 The canvas is not wide enough to stitch the complete design so two lengths will need to be pieced together. To do this, fold the length of canvas in half along the width and cut along the fold. Take one of the cut pieces and fold it in half along the length and cut along the fold. You should now have a large rectangle and two smaller rectangles.

2 Cut the selvedge off one edge of the large rectangle, then place the large rectangle and one smaller rectangle side by side on a flat surface with raw edges together. Overlap the raw edges by about 2.5cm (1in), then secure the two layers together using sewing thread and large cross stitches (see fig 10). The canvas is now ready to use.

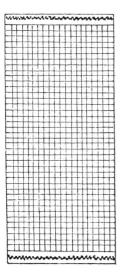
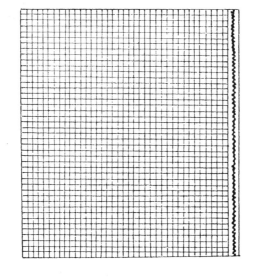
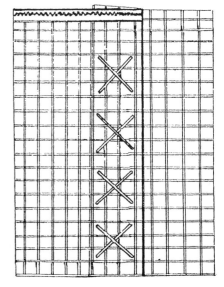

Fig 10   Joining canvas pieces

3 Prepare your canvas for work in the same way as for Aida or evenweave fabric, reading through the Techniques section if necessary and marking the centre point. The design is worked in cross stitch with one strand of tapestry wool (yarn). Use a large tapestry needle and a thimble to protect your fingers.

4 To work the rug design, refer to the charts on pages 110–113 and the photographs on page 104 and below as a reference. The chart shows the design used for the tiger stripes cushion. The central section on the chart forms one quarter of the central panel for the rug. You need to stitch this section four times to form the square that makes up the central panel of the rug. Next, work a border ten stitches wide all around the central square using black 7310.

5 Work the outer border using the border section charted on page 112. Begin at the top left-hand corner and keep repeating the border sections until you have completed one side of the rug, then repeat the process for the other three sides.

6 When the design is complete, trim away excess canvas to within 13cm (5in) of the stitches. Fold the canvas turnings to the back of the rug leaving one hole showing and one thread running across the top of the fold. Hand stitch the turnings in place.

7 Finish the rug by adding an overcast edging. Using two strands of black 7310, secure the thread at the back of the canvas, insert the needle into the hole nearest the cross stitches and pull to the front of the canvas. The overcast thread should share a hole with the last stitch of the cross stitch design. Take the needle to the back of the canvas and work the next stitch in the same way (see fig 2 page 17). Work two stitches in each hole to cover the canvas completely.

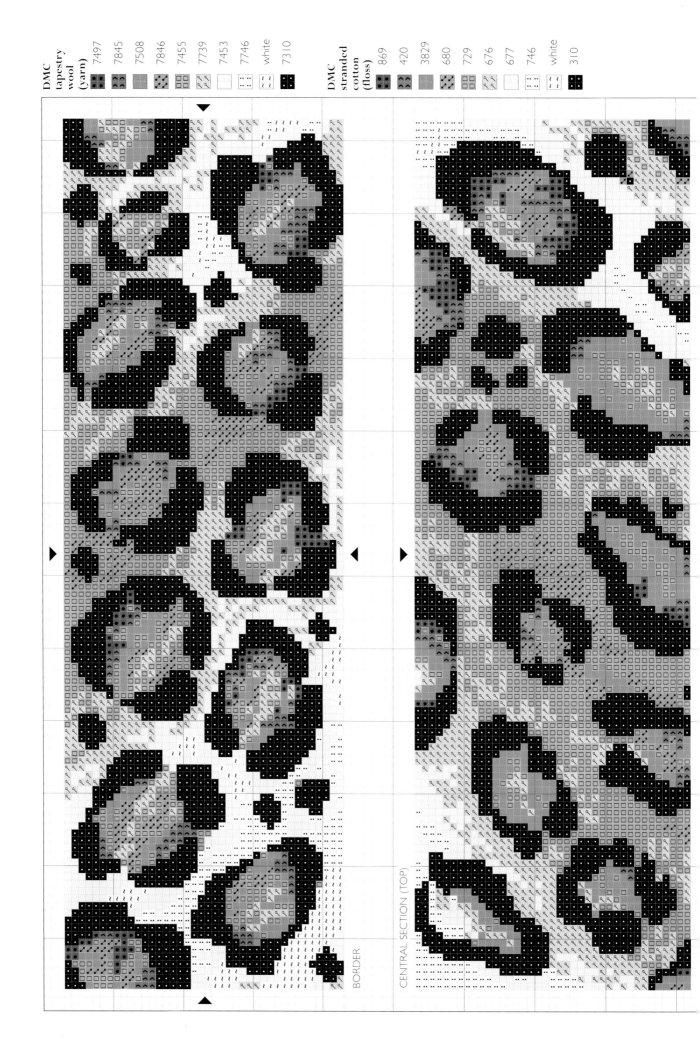

DMC tapestry wool (yarn)
7497 7845 7508 7846 7455 7739 7453 7746 white 7310

DMC stranded cotton (floss)
869 420 3829 680 729 676 677 746 white 310

BORDER

CENTRAL SECTION (TOP)

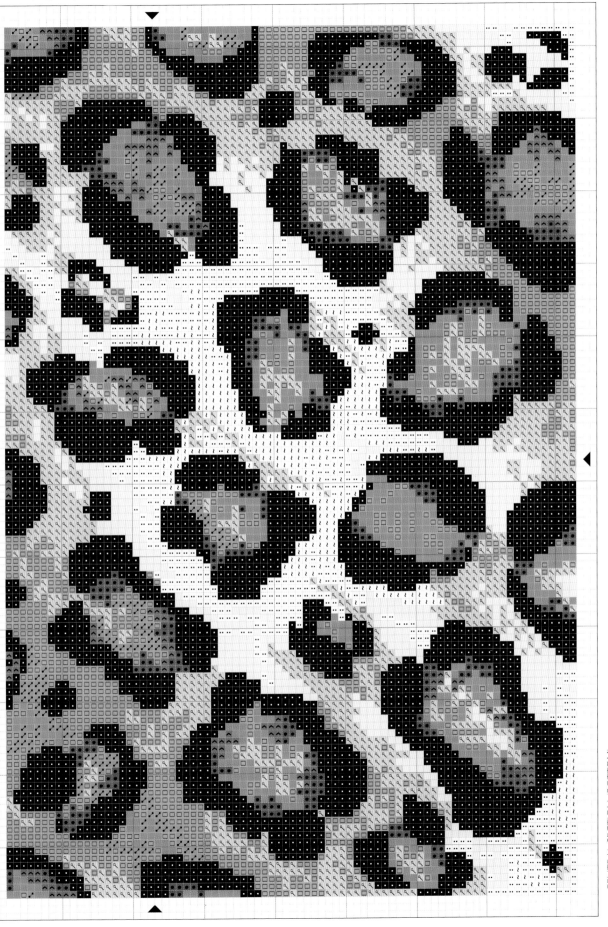

DMC
tapestry
wool
(yarn)

7459
7401
7922
7919
7918
7917
7739
7453
7746
white
7310

DMC
stranded
cotton
(floss)

300
975
3826
976
977
3827
676
677
746
white
310

BORDER

CENTRAL SECTION (TOP)

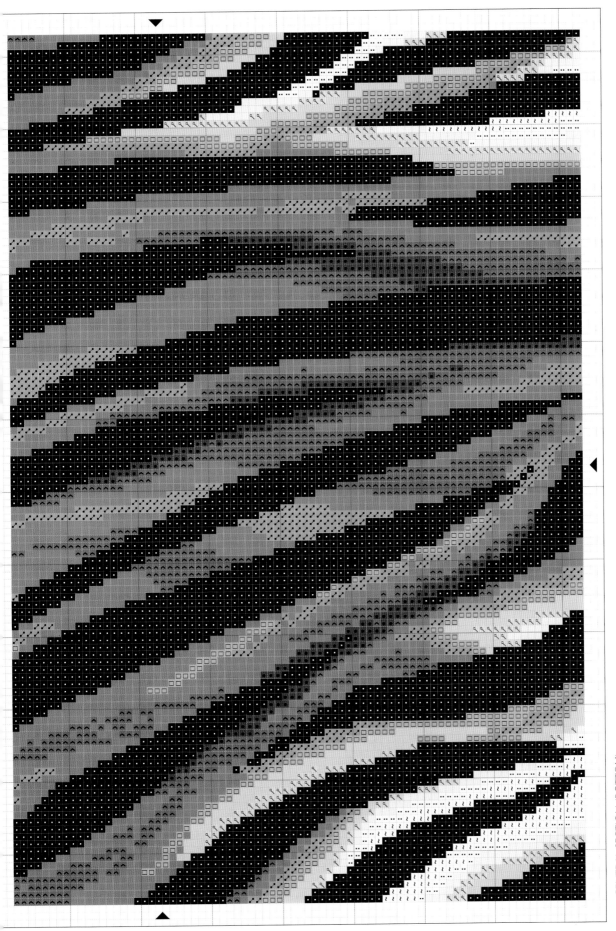

CENTRAL SECTION (BOTTOM)

Bright Eyes Footstool

This beautiful design is worked in a mixture of cross stitch, three-quarter cross stitch and backstitch and captures the appealing character of the beautiful Birman, with their sapphire blue eyes and pretty white feet. Birman are a cross between Siamese and Persian, combining the coloured tips of the Siamese and the fluffy coat of the Persian. We have stitched this design over two threads of a 28-count linen. It has been mounted into a footstool, however the design would be the same size if worked on a 14-count Aida over one block and would make a lovely picture.

FINISHED DESIGN SIZE

22 x 39cm (8¾ x 15¼in) approximately

WHAT YOU WILL NEED

• Dark blue 28-count Cashel linen (E3281), 43 x 56cm (17 x 22in)

• 33 x 46cm (13 x 18in) rectangular footstool (available from MacGregor Designs – see Stockists page 127)

1 Prepare your fabric, reading through the Techniques section if necessary and marking the centre point. Refer to the Stitch Guide on page 12 for how to work the stitches.

2 When stitching the design, use two strands of stranded cotton (floss) for the cross stitch and one for the backstitch, working over two fabric threads. Use one strand of stranded cotton to work the cross stitch for the shading in the foreground using med navy blue 311, dark baby blue 312 and dark baby blue 322.

3 Work the backstitch detail in black 310 around the eyes and for the eyebrow hairs. Use one strand of white to work the long stitches for the whiskers.

4 To mount the completed embroidery into the footstool, refer to the manufacturer's instructions.

DMC STRANDED COTTON (FLOSS)

I skein: white; black 310; med navy blue 311; dark baby blue 312; dark baby blue 322; black brown 3371; dark desert sand 3772; dark straw 3820; light straw 3822; hazelnut brown 3828; dark desert sand 407; dark hazelnut brown 420; light hazelnut brown 422; light beige brown 543; cream 712; light tan 738; light tan 739; dark topaz 781; dark topaz 782; med topaz 783; light blue 813; dark blue 825; med blue 826; light blue 827; light blue 828; dark beige brown 838; dark beige brown 839; light beige brown 841; light beige brown 842; dark hazelnut brown 869; dark parrot green 904; dark red copper 918; red copper 919; med copper 920; copper 921

THE BIRMAN

Birman are considered to be sacred cats and there are several ancient legends describing the origin of these beautiful creatures. One describes an attack on an ancient Burmese temple where the high priest was injured. The temple cats sensed that he was dying and as he died his favourite cat jumped onto him and was transformed into a Birman. Where the cat's paws touched the priest's body, the fur remained white, symbolising goodness. It is thought that each time a Birman cat dies, the soul of a priest accompanies it to heaven.

DMC stranded cotton (floss)

827		3371		420		739		543		919		782		904
828		825		738			842		918		783		3822
white		826		839		422		841		407		921		3820
310		813		838		3828		712		3772		920		781
311		312		322									

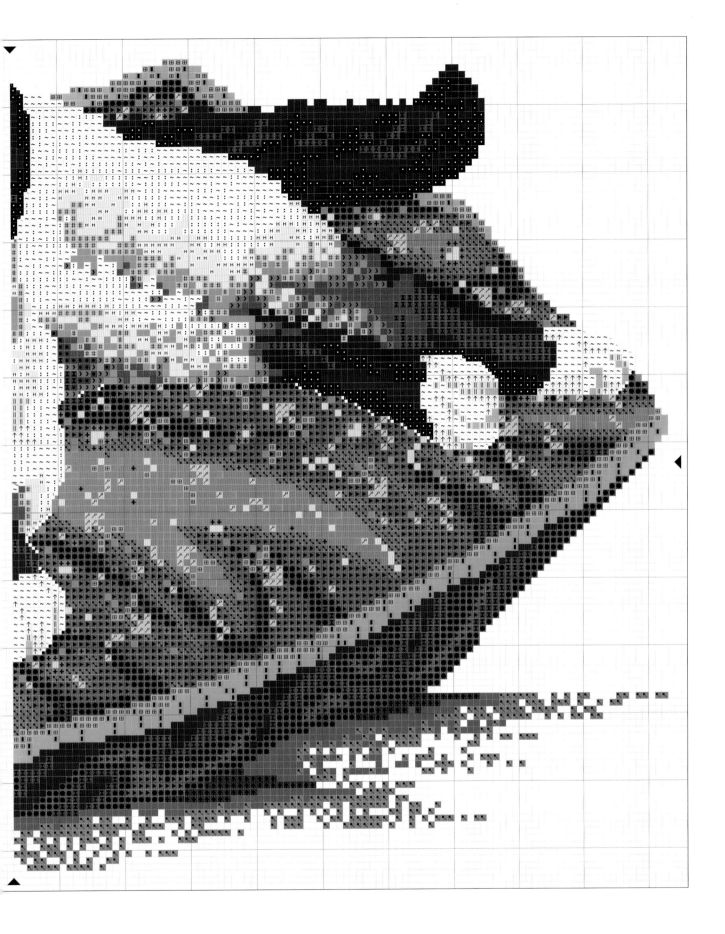

Gifts for Kids and Cats

This collection of cute designs has been used to create a selection of gifts not only for children but for cats as well! We hope these versatile little designs will provide you with hours of enjoyment and inspiration. As they use just whole cross stitch they are ideal for beginners and children too. A variety of fabrics are used to work the designs – from Aida for the catnip toys, mug and pencil holder, to perforated paper for the ruler and waste canvas for the fleece bean-bag bed and scarf. The T-shirt can be bought ready prepared with a panel for embroidery.

DMC STRANDED COTTON (FLOSS)

Siamese kitten

I skein: black 310; white; light golden brown 434; tan 436; cream 712; light tan 738; dark coffee brown 938

Work a French knot in white for the eye highlight

Flower border

I skein: dark lemon 444; dark electric blue 995; light Christmas green 703

Work backstitch detail using light Christmas green 703 for the flower stems

Mouse

I skein: black 310; white; light peach 353; med golden brown 433; light golden brown 434; light golden brown 435; tan 436; light tan 437; light tan 738; light coffee brown 801; dark coffee brown 938

Work a French knot in white for the eye highlight

Goldfish

I skein: black 310; white; tangerine 740; med tangerine 741; light tangerine 742; med yellow 743; dark burnt orange 900; med burnt orange 946; burnt orange 947

Work backstitch detail in black 310 around the eye and a French knot using white for the eye highlight

Paw prints (small, medium and large)

I skein: black 310; plus other yarn colours, stated in the relevant projects

SIAMESE KITTEN T-SHIRT

FINISHED DESIGN SIZE

Siamese kitten, flower border and paw prints, 6.5 x 25.5cm (2¹/₂ x 10in) approximately

WHAT YOU WILL NEED

- T-shirt for embroidery (available from Framecraft – see Stockists page 127)

DMC STRANDED COTTON (FLOSS)

Use the thread list for the Siamese kitten, flower border and paw prints left

1 Prepare your fabric, reading through the Techniques section if necessary. Refer to the Stitch Guide on page 12 for how to work the stitches.

2 Follow the charts on pages 125 and 126 and work the Siamese kitten, then work the flower border along the bottom edge of the design. Finally, stitch a selection of different sized paw prints using black 310, light tangerine 742 and burnt orange 947 (see photograph opposite). Use two strands of stranded cotton (floss) for the cross stitch and one for the backstitch and French knots. Refer to each design thread list (left) for details on backstitch and French knots.

PAW PRINT SCARF

FINISHED DESIGN SIZE

18cm (7in) square approximately

WHAT YOU WILL NEED

- 8-count waste canvas, 25cm (10in) square
- Polyester fleece fabric 30 x 150cm (12 x 60in) wide

DMC STRANDED COTTON (FLOSS)

Use the thread list for the Siamese kitten on page 118, plus white for the paw prints

1 Prepare your fabric, reading through the Techniques section if necessary. Refer to the Stitch Guide on page 12 for how to work the stitches and to page 10 for Using Waste Canvas. Pin and tack (baste) the waste canvas 10cm (4in) from one end of the fleece scarf.

2 Follow the charts on pages 125/126 and use six strands of stranded cotton (floss) to work the cross stitch. Work the Siamese kitten, then use white to work a selection of paw prints in various sizes to the side and above the kitten (see photograph page 119).

3 When the stitching is complete remove the waste canvas threads, leaving the embroidered stitches on the fleece fabric (see Using Waste Canvas page 10). Press the fabric from the wrong side, then finish the scarf by cutting a 5cm (2in) fringe at each end.

SIAMESE KITTEN MUG

FINISHED DESIGN SIZE

7.5 x 24cm (3 x 9½in) approximately

WHAT YOU WILL NEED

- White 14-count Aida, 19 x 28cm (7½ x 11in)
- Mug for embroidery (available from Framecraft — see Stockists page 127)

DMC STRANDED COTTON (FLOSS)

Use the thread list for the Siamese kitten and flower border on page 118

1 Prepare your fabric, reading through the Techniques section if necessary. Refer to the Stitch Guide on page 12 for how to work the stitches.

2 Draw a rectangle in pencil onto the Aida fabric, to a size that will fit your mug — ours measured 9 x 25cm (3½ x 9¾in). Follow the charts and stitch a row of kittens along the centre of the design area, and a flower border at the top and bottom edges (see picture opposite). Use two strands of stranded cotton (floss) for the cross stitch and one for the backstitch and French knots. Refer to each design thread list for details on adding backstitch and French knots.

3 To complete your mug follow the manufacturer's instructions.

CATS AT PLAY

Play is important for cats, teaching them to use and develop their skills. Kittens start to play at about five weeks old and are soon running around the house, climbing curtains and pouncing on anything that moves. Cats continue to play into adulthood.

PAW PRINT RULER

FINISHED DESIGN SIZE

Medium paw print 1.5cm (⅝in) square approximately

WHAT YOU WILL NEED

- Ruler and paper for embroidery (available from Framecraft – see Stockists, page 127)

DMC STRANDED COTTON (FLOSS)

Use the thread list for the paw prints in step 2 (right)

1 Prepare your fabric, reading through the Techniques section if necessary. Refer to the Stitch Guide on page 12 for how to work the stitches.

2 Follow the medium paw print chart on page 125 and use one strand of stranded cotton (floss) for the cross stitch. Work on the perforated paper using a mixture of black 310, dark lemon 444, dark olive green 730 and dark electric blue 995 (see photograph below).

3 To complete your ruler follow the manufacturer's instructions.

PAW PRINT PEN HOLDER

FINISHED DESIGN SIZE
Siamese kitten, flower border and paw prints 8.5 x 23.5cm (3¼ x 9¼in) approximately

WHAT YOU WILL NEED
- White 14-count Aida, 23 x 38cm (9 x 15in)
- Pen holder for embroidery (available from Framecraft – see Stockists page 127)

DMC STRANDED COTTON (FLOSS)
Use the thread list for Siamese kitten, flower border and paw prints on page 118

1 Prepare your fabric, reading through the Techniques section if necessary. To work out where to stitch the designs, measure the length and sides of the pen holder and draw this shape onto a piece of Aida – ours measured 9 x 25cm (3½ x 9¾in). Refer to the Stitch Guide on page 12 for how to work the stitches.

2 Stitch a Siamese kitten at the centre of your design with paw prints on either side and finish off with a flower border at the top and bottom edges (see photograph page 121). Follow the charts using two strands of stranded cotton (floss) for the cross stitch and one for the backstitch and French knot. Refer to each design thread list for details on adding backstitch and French knots.

3 To complete your pen holder follow the manufacturer's instructions.

BEAN-BAG BED

FINISHED DESIGN SIZE
Goldfish 9 x 15cm (3½ x 6in)
Mouse 6.5 x 11.5cm (2½ x 4½in)
Siamese kitten 7.5 x 9cm (3 x 3½in)
Large paw print 4cm (1¾in) square

WHAT YOU WILL NEED
- 8-count waste canvas, 1m x 68cm (1⅛yd x 27in) wide
- Polyester fleece fabric 1m x 150cm (1⅛yd x 60in)
- Calico for lining 1m x 150cm (1⅛yd x 60in) wide
- Polystyrene balls for filling, 1 cubic ft
- Thick brown wool for mouse tail
- Matching sewing thread

DMC STRANDED COTTON (FLOSS)
Use the thread lists for the goldfish, mouse, Siamese kitten and large paw print on page 118, or chose your own combination of designs

1 Before you start stitching the bean-bag design you will need to cut out the fleece fabric. Draw a template of the bean-bag pattern (see fig 11, page 124) referring to Using Graphs on page 10 for instructions.

2 Using the pattern, cut two shapes each from calico and fleece. For the bean-bag sides, cut two 28 x 82cm (11 x 32¼in) strips each from calico and fleece. Place the fleece strips together with right sides facing, then pin and stitch the strips together along the short edges to form a fabric loop. Repeat for the calico strips.

3 Read through the Techniques section if necessary and refer to the Stitch Guide on page 12 for how to work the stitches and page 10 for Using Waste Canvas. Cut two 23 x 80cm (9 x 31½in) strips of waste canvas, then pin and tack (baste) these strips in place on the right side of the joined fleece strips, to cover the whole area of the fleece fabric.

4 Choose which designs you want to stitch on your bean-bag and, following the relevant charts on page 125/126, work these randomly around the fleece fabric (see photograph page 123). Use six strands of stranded cotton (floss) for the cross stitch and two for the backstitch and French knots. Refer to each design thread list for details on backstitch and French knots.

5 When the stitching is complete remove the waste canvas threads, leaving the embroidered stitches on the fleece fabric (refer to Using Waste Canvas page 10). Press the fabric from the wrong side. Stitch a 7cm (2³⁄₄in) length of brown wool to the mouse's bottom for its tail.

TO MAKE THE BEAN-BAG BED

1 Take the two calico ovals and the joined calico strip to make the lining. The calico strip forms the bean-bag side and the oval shapes form the top and base.

2 Carefully pin and tack (baste) the top shape to the side section, matching the notches with the side seams. Machine stitch in place. Repeat with the base section but leave a 25cm (10in) gap for turning. Turn the lining bag through to the right side.

3 Repeat this process for the fleece bean-bag cover. Insert the calico lining into the bean-bag cover, then carefully fill the calico lining shape with polystyrene balls. Use strong hand stitches to close the gap in the calico lining bag. Finally, secure the gap in the fleece cover with slipstitches.

CATS NEED PLAY

Because we feed our cats regularly, domestic cats have lots of surplus energy as they don't have to worry about going out to hunt for their dinner. If this surplus energy is not used in a positive way your cat may become frustrated and destructive. This explains why you may find your cat chewing your plants, scratching your furniture, carpets or wallpaper, running up your curtains or having a mad half hour. To prevent these problems ensure that your cat is always mentally stimulated and has plenty of opportunity for exercise. Toys provide the perfect solution to this problem. Cats of all ages love to play with toys and those that make a noise or are filled with catnip are of particular interest to them.

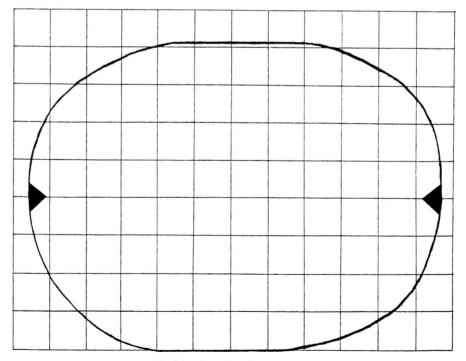

Fig 11   Bean-bag bed template

CATNIP TOYS

FINISHED DESIGN SIZES

5 x 10cm (2 x 4in) approximately

WHAT YOU WILL NEED

- White 11-count Aida, 20cm (8in) square, for mouse and goldfish
- Felt for backing
- Lightweight polyester wadding (batting)
- Dried catnip
- Thick brown wool for mouse tail
- Matching sewing thread

DMC STRANDED COTTON (FLOSS)

Use the thread lists for the mouse and goldfish on page 118

1 Prepare your fabric, reading through the Techniques section if necessary and referring to the Stitch Guide on page 12 for working the stitches.

2 Use four strands of stranded cotton (floss) for the cross stitch and two strands for the backstitch and French knots. Refer to each design thread list for details on working backstitch and French knots.

3 Following the charts on page 126 and with reference to the photograph on page 123, work your chosen design, then trim away excess fabric to within 6mm (¼in) of the completed design. Cut a piece of felt to the same size.

4 With right sides facing, pin, tack (baste) and then machine stitch the front and back pieces together, stitching close to the embroidered stitches and leaving a gap for turning. Turn the shape through to right side, fill with wadding (batting) and dried catnip, then secure the opening with slipstitches.

5 To finish the mouse, make a tail by cutting a 6.5cm (2½in) length of brown wool, and hand stitch it to the mouse's bottom.

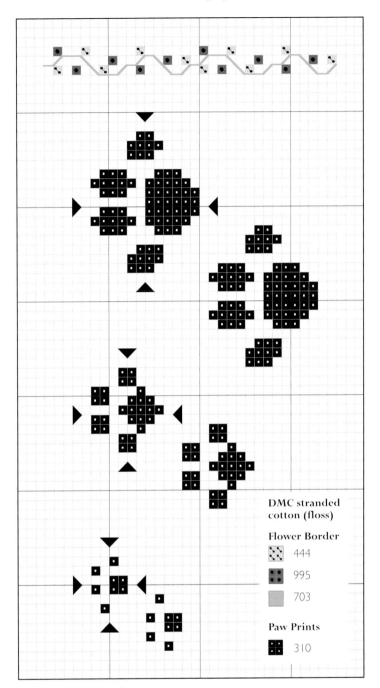

DMC stranded
cotton (floss)

Flower Border

▨	444
▦	995
▢	703

Paw Prints

▦	310

Gifts for Kids and Cats

DMC stranded cotton (floss)

Goldfish

743
742
741
740
947
946
900
white
310

DMC stranded cotton (floss)

Mouse

353
738
437
436
435
434
433
801
938
white
310

DMC stranded cotton (floss)

Siamese Kitten

712
738
436
434
938
white
310

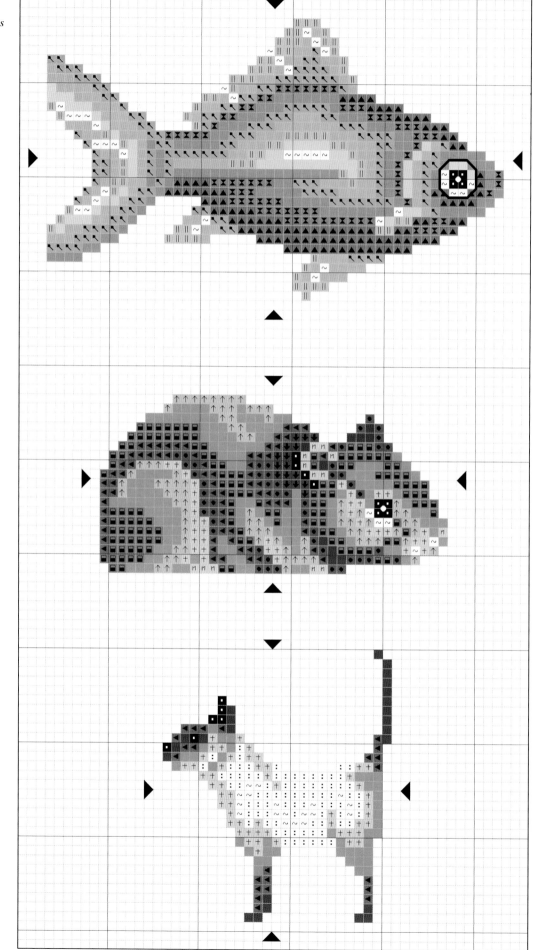

STOCKISTS

If you should require any further information about products, catalogues, price lists or local stockists from any of the suppliers mentioned, contact them direct by post or phone. Please remember to always include a stamped-addressed envelope. If contacting them by phone, they will be able to tell you if there is any charge for the catalogue or price lists.

DMC Creative World, Pullman Road, Wigston, Leicester LE18 2DY. Tel: 0116 281 1040.
For all threads and embroidery fabrics used throughout the book and for the name and address of your nearest DMC and Zweigart stockist.

DMC threads are supplied in the USA by: The DMC Corporation, South Hackensack Ave, Port Kearny, Building 10A, South Kearny, NJ 07032-4688.
www.dmc-usa.com

Zweigart fabric is supplied in the USA by: Joan Toggitt Ltd. 2 Riverview Drive, Somerset, NJ 08873-1139.
E-mail: info@zweigart.com
www.zweigart.com

Framecraft Miniatures Ltd, 372-376 Summer Lane, Hockley, Birmingham B19 3QA. Tel: 0121 212 0551.
Suppliers of the oval wooden tray, silver teaspoon, jam pot cover, bell pull hanging rods, desk accessories, mug and baby's T-shirt.

Framecraft products are also supplied worldwide by: Anne Brinkley Designs Inc, 761 Palmer Avenue, Holmdel, NJ 97733, USA.
Gay Bowles Sales Inc, PO Box 1060, Janesville, WI 53547, USA.
Ireland Needlecraft Pty Ltd, 4, 2-4 Keppel Drive, Hallam, Vic 3803, Australia.

MacGregor Designs, PO Box 129, Burton upon Trent, DE14 3XH. Tel: 01283 702117.
For mail order catalogue of specialist woodwork accessories. Suppliers of the rectangular footstool for the Bright Eyes design.

Fred Aldous Ltd, PO Box 135, 37 Lever Street, Manchester M1 1LW. Tel: 0161 236 2477. Fax: 0161 236 6075. E-mail: Aldous@btinternet.com
Suppliers of calico and polystyrene balls for the bean-bag bed.

Market Square (Warminster) Ltd, Wing Farm, Longbridge Deverill, Warminster, Wilts BA12 7DD. Tel: 01985 841042.
Source for the fire screen used with the serval cat design.

Vilene products were used on projects throughout the book. A selection of iron-on interfacings is available in major department stores and all good haberdashery shops.

Some of the designs included in this book are available in kit form by mail. For further details contact: The Janlynn Corporation, 34 Front Street, PO Box 51848, Indian Orchard, MA 01151 – 5848, USA. At time of publication, Sitting Pretty, Lion Cubs, Leopard, Tiger, Lion Territory and Cats in a Row were available in kit form.

ACKNOWLEDGEMENTS
We would both like to give a special thank you to our very long suffering husbands, Ian and Tim, for all their support whilst Jayne and I worked more frantically than ever on this book. Thank you to the following people for their contributions and help with getting this book published: Doreen Montgomery, Cheryl Brown and Kay Ball at David & Charles and Di Lewis for the wonderful photography. Thank you also to Cara Ackerman, Sarah Gray, Gleyns Black-Roberts and Susan Haigh and to John Parkes of Outpost Trading.

INDEX